Awesome Projects from Unexpected Places

Awesome Projects from Unexpected Places

Bottle Cap Tables, Tree Branch Coat Racks, Cigar Box Guitars, and Other Cool Ideas for You and Your Home

Instructables.com
Edited and Introduced by Noah Weinstein

Skyhorse Publishing

Skyhorse Publishing books may be purchased in bulk at special discounts for sales promotion, corporate gifts, fund-raising, or educational purposes. Special editions can also be created to specifications. For details, contact the Special Sales Department, Skyhorse Publishing, 307 West 36th Street, 11th Floor, New York, NY 10018 or info@skyhorsepublishing.com.

Skyhorse® and Skyhorse Publishing® are registered trademarks of Skyhorse Publishing, Inc.®, a Delaware corporation.

www.skyhorsepublishing.com

10 9 8 7 6 5 4 3 2 1

Library of Congress Cataloging-in-Publication Data is available on file.

ISBN: 978-1-62087-705-0

Printed in China

Disclaimer:

This book is intended to offer general guidance. It is sold with the understanding that every effort was made to provide the most current and accurate information. However, errors and omissions are still possible. Any use or misuse of the information contained herein is solely the responsibility of the user, and the author and publisher make no warrantees or claims as to the truth or validity of the information. The author and publisher shall have neither liability nor responsibility to any person or entity with respect to any loss or damage caused, or alleged to have been caused, directly or indirectly, by the information contained in this book. Furthermore, this book is not intended to give professional dietary, technical, or medical advice. Please refer to and follow any local laws when using any of the information contained herein, and act responsibly and safely at all times.

Table of Contents

table of contents

Introduction

The makers of the projects included in this book have repurposed and reused everyday items to create unique furnishings for their homes and meaningful gifts for others. Equipped with the vision to not only see the latent potential and beauty in common items, but also the skills necessary to transform those objects into creative and new applications, these projects are at the core of the maker movement and can inspire us all. Awesome Projects from Unexpected Places contains thirty-three projects you can make for your living room, kitchen, and backyard, with step-by-step instructions to help you follow along, or to inspire you to make and share an awesome project of your own.

All of the projects in this book are from Instructables.com. Instructables is the most popular project-sharing community on the Internet, and part of the Autodesk family of creative communities. Since August 2005, Instructables has provided easy publishing tools to enable passionate, creative people to share their most innovative projects, recipes, skills, and ideas. Instructables has over 90,000 projects covering all subjects, including crafts, art, electronics, kids, home improvement, pets, outdoors, reuse, bikes, cars, robotics, food, decorating, woodworking, games, and more.

*Special thanks to Instructables Interactive Designer Gary Lu for the Instructables Robot illustrations!

Section 1
Furnish

Bottle Cap Table with Resin-Poured Surface

By americangypsy
(http://www.instructables
.com/id/Bottle-Cap-Table-with-
Poured-Resin-Surface/)

We've been collecting bottle caps for what seems like forever anticipating this table. After moving our collection with us to four different homes in three different states, we now have enough caps for this table, plus a few matching stools. What makes this project different from a simple mosaic project is that we covered the table with a thick resin, creating a look quite similar to the tables at your favorite pub.

Step 1: Collect Bottle Caps
Tips
- Become friends with bartenders.
- Have a cheap date night.
- Visit alleys behind local bars.
- Buy microbrews based on how cool the caps are, not how good the beer is.
- Get your friends to help you collect.

- When traveling overseas, buy beer instead of souvenirs.

Step 2: Find the Table
You can do this on any sized surface. I've seen huge bars covered in pennies or old photos, but unless you want to deal with storing wheelbarrows of bottle caps, a bistro-sized or small end table is good for starters. We used a Noresund IKEA table purchased in the As Is area at our local IKEA. I believe it is now discontinued. Sorry.

Step 3: Lay Out Your Design
We started out with a random design, featuring just one bottle cap from every kind we had in our cap stash. This left room for some repeats, so we arranged a pattern around the circular shape of the table.

3

Step 4: Begin Gluing

You might be thinking that you can just lay caps down and pour resin over them, but don't skip this step. Since we were covering our table with clear resin, we weren't too concerned with the type of glue used. I started out with contact cement, moved on to furniture glue, then Liquid Nails for small projects, and even tried siliconized caulk. I ended up using plain old super glue. This was the best option and the one I suggest for you. Since the caps are going to get covered with resin, they just need to stick to the table, so a couple of dots are all you need. Don't go crazy, because messy excess glue will show through the resin when you're done.

Extra information regarding this step: Although I suggest super glue for this project, the contact cement was truly the strongest adhesive. However, it took some time to use and was less forgiving. The silicone-based glues (Liquid Nails and caulk) seemed to shift or expand as it dried, which ultimately threw our design off. Super glue was the least elegant choice, but it dries relatively quickly and was rigid enough for this project. **One note of caution:** I discovered that Super Glue reacts with the hexane/toluene base of contact cement. They discolor and create a crystalline growth that resembles a fuzzy, white mold that must be removed with acetone. So pick one type of glue and go with it to avoid this kind of situation.

Step 5: Prepare Your Surface

Once everything was glued down, I used blue painter's tape to cover the edge of my table just even with the surface of the table. This is usually recommended to avoid drips of resin from drying to sides of your project, but I did it to keep the duct tape from getting my table all sticky (see Step 6). Don't forget to also tape up any holes on the surface of your table. I did this from underneath so that the blue tape wouldn't show once the resin was applied. If you have a table surface with lots of openings (like a metal mesh or expanded metal), you may want to get a piece of Plexiglas or MDF and use that for your tabletop.

Step 6: Build a Barrier

If your table has a rim, you can skip this step. Since mine had no rim, I had to create a way to keep the resin at a depth that would cover the bottle caps without running off the side. I needed something sticky enough that it would create a barrier against resin, yet slick enough that it would not stick to the resin.

I decided to use aluminum foil and duct tape. First, cut some long strips of duct tape to go around the edge of the table. Next, cut strips of foil about 3" wide and 1" longer than your strips of duct tape. Laying the strips of duct tape sticky side up, carefully cover about half of the duct tape with a strip of foil. See photo for details. The straighter you do this, the better. You could also do this with wide painter's tape and eliminate the need to cover the edges of the table with painter's tape in Step 5.

Tape the foil/tape strips around the edge of the table, making sure that the bottom edge of the foil falls just below the surface of the tabletop (the actual table, not the bottle caps). See the photo for details. The reason: If the sticky surface of the duct tape is above the tabletop, the resin will stick to it and defeat the purpose of making an easy-release barrier. If the foil is too far below the tabletop, resin may seep over the edge, trapping blue tape underneath.

Step 7: Cover with Resin

I won't get into how to mix the resin since there are instructions in the box, not to mention ample tutorials available online. The resin I used was Envirotex Lite Pour-on High Gloss Finish. You will, however, need to spread the resin to get into the gaps between the bottle caps as well as out to the edges. This is why your caps need to be glued down, as you will be running a rigid piece of paper or plastic over the surface of the caps. This is a great opportunity to use those fake credit cards that come in your junk mail. I used an old insurance card, but any stiff plastic or cardboard would suffice. Remember that the resin will level itself out, so just make sure you have enough to fill in the gaps and even out any high areas. You may want to cover your work to keep any random hairs or dust from getting stuck. Now walk away for about seven or eight hours.

Step 8: Remove the Tape

After the resin is fully set, carefully begin peeling away the foil/tape. If the foil was kept relatively smooth and the tape was not touching the resin, it should peel away from the hardened resin easily. The only time I had problems was when some resin seeped between overlapping ends of the foil/tape. Also, there were a couple of spots where the

5

resin seeped over the edge of the blue tape slightly. These were both easily remedied using a hobby knife.

Step 9: And Voila!

You have a great new conversation piece for your home or patio.

Wine Barrel Beer Table

By Warrick Smith

(liquidhandwash)

(http://www.instructables.com/
id/Wine-Barrel-Beer-Table/)

I found half a wine barrel that the local pub was throwing out, so I grabbed it because it was made out of oak, and I would hate to see that in someone's fireplace.

Step 1: The Barrel

The half-barrel that I found was almost ready to fall to pieces. Two of the bands had fallen off and the top one was also ready to fall off. It would be very difficult to reassemble, so I carefully put the bands back on and took it home.

I was not sure what to make until I saw the nice graphics on the top, so I sanded the top back and put furniture oil on it. It looked good, so I decided to keep the graphic, which would mean keeping the top intact. My first thought was a coffee table. But as the project progressed, the misses said she liked the height of the table and would like it on the deck next to her chair.

Step 2: Stuff You Will Need
- Sandpaper grits 40, 80, 120, 240
- Matt black paint
- 3 or 4 coach bolts with washers and nuts
- Drill and dill bits
- 3 or 4 wood screws
- Small nail or tacks
- Hammer
- Jig saw (reciprocating saw)
- Clean rags
- Your favorite timber finish
- Angle grinder, with sanding disc
- About 2 hours
- Beer

Step 3: Mark Out the Legs

I decided to make the table with three legs, as they don't rock around on

furnish

uneven surfaces, so I marked out the three slats that were going to be used for legs. I then made sure the bands were straight and tight and then drilled and screwed the three slates to the bottom band so nothing would move in the next steps.

Step 4: Remove the Sharp Bits

The top band had quite a sharp edge on it, so I used a grinder with a sanding disc to remove the edge and make it smooth.

Step 5: Remove the Bands and Paint

I removed the top two bands with a hammer and a block of wood and then cleaned them with thinners. I hung them from the roof with wire and spray painted matt black. I also painted the heads of the coach bolts.

Step 6: Sanding

I used four different grit sandpapers starting with 40, then 80, 120, and 240. I only sanded the top and the top of the sides and the legs. Sanding is boring so I got some free child labor to do most of it.

Step 8: Refit the Top Band

I put the top band back on and knocked it down with a hammer.

Step 7: Oiling

You could probably do this step last, but I put a coat of my favorite furniture oil on early so it would be under the bands, helping protect the timber from spills and moisture. Just use a rag to rub the oil on.

Step 9: Cut Out the Legs

Next, I drilled three holes big enough for my jig saw blade to pass through and cut around the bottom of the line that the second band had left. I found that oak was very hard and difficult to cut with a dull blade. I should really have put a new blade in the saw, but the store was closed. Don't forget to leave the legs uncut. The waste wood can then be removed.

9

Step 10: Fitting the Second Band

The second band can now be fitted. I knocked it down with a hammer and a block of wood and drilled three holes through the band and the legs, into which the coach bolts were fitted. To help keep the top band in place, I drilled three small holes and nailed in some carpet tacks that had an old style black head, which matched the look of the table.

Step 11: Remove the Bottom Band

Now that the table has been bolted together, the bottom band can be removed and the legs sanded and finished off. The misses likes the height of the table, but it could be cut down for a coffee table.

furnish

Step 12: Other stuff

I think, now that it's finished, it would look better with four legs, and it needs to be a bit shorter, as the curve on the end of the legs make it look a bit odd. But it is very stable, doesn't rock around, and the ring around the top stops my drunk friends from putting their glasses on the edge of the table, which always inevitably leads to their beers getting knocked over.

Recycled Tire Coffee Table

By Adam White (bigern00)
(http://www.instructables.com/
id/Recycled-Tire-Coffee-Table/)

Repurposing my used truck tire into furniture was a great way to put a durable, used item to work for another lifetime.

We haven't had a coffee table for a couple years. My need for one and my desire to build one met up one day while I was surfing the Internet. I read a blurb about someone who made an ottoman out of two stacked tires and suddenly my weekend now had purpose.

My wife likes the tire look for now, but there are plans for an elastic cover with remote control pockets on the perimeter in the works. The best part is that the top lifts off and there is a ton of storage inside the tire. The leg supports effectively divide the interior space up inside and make it easier to organize, too.

Step 1: Tools and Materials

I bounced around the shop on this project a bit due to its prototypical nature, but it could have been built with far fewer tools and had the same or better outcome if I had more experience working with tires (which I do, now).

Power Tools
- Table saw
- Drill press
- Band saw
- Lathe
- Router (table mounted)
- Router (handheld)
- Belt sander
- Disc sander
- Jigsaw
- Drill
- Impact driver

Hand Tools
- Wrenches/sockets
- Screwdrivers
- Sanding block
- Hammer
- Mallet
- Pencils/markers
- Hand plane

Materials
- Old tire in need of repurposing
- ½ sheet plywood
- Threaded rod
- Assorted wood screws
- 3 lag screws
- Assorted washers
- Stain or paint

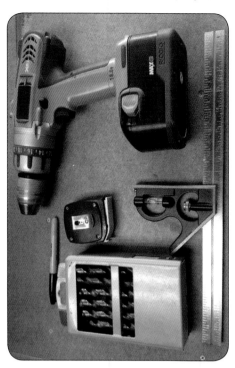

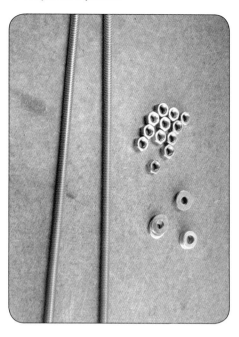

Step 2: Layout

I'm a fan of three-legged things. The stability of the tripod means you don't have to worry much about solid footing on any surface (like a slightly off-level tile floor).

Before working with the tire, you will benefit from giving it a good scrub-down with soapy water and a stiff brush to remove brake dust and any road kill remnants that may be lingering. I got a small pick and pulled the tiny pebbles and glass chunks out of the tread, as well.

Now that you're tire is clean, let's move on to layout. For the tripod, you will have to divide the tire into three even sections. An Internet search can answer any questions you have, but I summarized the two most helpful circle geometry theorems in the picture to help out.

Once you have laid out the thirds on the inside rim of the tire, use a square (as pictured) to transfer the marks to the opposite side.

furnish

Dividing a Circle into Thirds

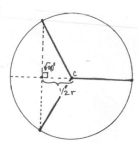

① draw a chord through the center

② go ½ the radius from the center and draw a perpendicular line

③ where the perp. line crosses circle are other two points

Finding the Center of a Circle (Thales' Theorem)

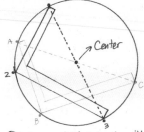

① Draw a right triangle with points on circumference, hypotenuse is a diameter chord

② repeat at a different angle

③ intersection of diameters is the center point of the circle

Step 3: I'm So Tired
Support Rods
With the thirds laid out on the inner bead, drill a hole for the support rods.

Shop Notes
- Rubber doesn't retain its shape when drilled, so for a ⁵⁄₁₆" threaded rod, you should use at least a ⁷⁄₁₆" bit, otherwise you will have hell getting it to fit.
- Go slowly when cutting and drilling to prevent heat build-up. Heat is the biggest killer of bits and blades: Don't go faster than the speed you would use to screw in a drill.
- Remember that tires have fibers, wires, metal, and other internal structure(s) most people don't think about. You will encounter them when you start drilling/cutting into the rubber.

I didn't measure the distance from the inside of the bead; I placed them at the same valley on the bead all the way around.

Insert the threaded rod through the holes. I cut the rod long enough to accommodate a nut, lock washer, and flat washer on each end. I suggest adding about ⅜" to this length to make it easier to get the floor supports on later. The round washers pulled on the sidewall of the tire and made a weird tension line. I clipped the flat washer so that it didn't dig into the sidewall and the problem was fixed.

Leg Holes
Draw the division lines out onto the sidewall. Halfway between the bead and tread on this line is where I put the leg holes. I could have had the legs mounted to the outside of the tire, but I wanted them to appear as if they grew out of the tire. It produced a cleaner look that I was going for.

Choose a hole saw that is a little bigger than the diameter of the legs you are going to use for the same reasons as above. If you need to clean up any slop around the holes you just made, a razor blade works great.

furnish

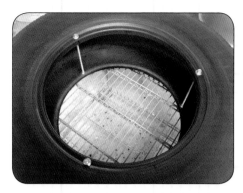

Step 4: She Got Legs

Okay, I understand most people don't have a lathe. I also understand that if someone does have a lathe, there is an 86.4 percent chance they are better at it than I am. I'm in the other 13.6 percent.

But I do have a lathe hanging around the shop, and I wanted to put a slight taper on the legs to give this chunky table slender legs, à la 1950s furniture. As for wood selection, this table is built out of leftovers, except for the top. The legs are turned out of a stick of Lyptus I had in my supplies. Later you will see the legs blackened to match our dark bookcases.

I cut the three legs apart on the table saw (be sure to support the taper to keep the leg from falling when free from the other piece). I set my miter sled to about a 2.5° and trimmed the top of each leg. This makes the legs splay out a little bit (an aesthetic decision mostly).

The gist of this leg design is to have the legs protrude through the tire. Each leg is attached to a plate. These plates are screwed to a stack of plywood (see next step) that has been cut to the profile of the tire interior, transferring the load around the whole tire instead of on just one sidewall. It is necessary to break this leg assembly up into two parts: leg plus plate and plywood stack. If you join them prior to getting them in place, it just won't fit and you will be fighting the tire.

Shop Notes

It didn't occur to me how pliable tire sidewalls were when they weren't inflated. My first go at this didn't have the stacked plywood leg mounts and the table felt like a jelly fish. After correcting that, it is solid.

I drilled a pilot hole into the top of each leg so I wouldn't split it during attachment. I don't have a chuck on my lathe, so I clamped them on my drill press.

Next, you will want to make a cardboard profile pattern of the "entire" interior (just terrible).

Shop Notes

For this example, cardboard is better than corrugated. If you don't know the difference, cardboard is on the back of a pad of paper, corrugated is used in bigger boxes. I used corrugated and about halfway through wondered why I didn't use plain cardboard. The corrugations made it more difficult to cut and I find it harder to trace around.

Transfer the pattern onto the end of some 1" × 4" of hardwood stock (I think the scrap I used was Alder) that is approximately three times longer than a top plate. Use the belt sander (very noisy, dusty option) or a hand plane (the quiet, no-dust option) to trim the board to match the profile. Contrary to the way I marked the board in the photo, you should leave a flat spot on the bottom of the plate where the leg will attach so they will have a stable joint.

After shaping the board, I cut it into the three support plates, then pre-drilled a pilot hole. I used a Forstner bit to recess the lag bolt head into the plate so it wouldn't interfere with the stack support. I attached the legs to their support plates using a 4" lag bolt (probably overkill, but it is what I had on hand).

Step 5: Wide, Wide World of Supports

Shop Notes

MDF is a good option for making patterns that are easy to reproduce. It shapes easily, it cuts easily, and it is cheap relative to wood. The downside to working with MDF is it is very dusty. This is just an annoyance if you follow safety protocol (dust mask or respiration), but if you do not wear breathing protection, you are inhaling the fibers *and* the formaldehyde-based adhesives they used to bond the board together. Just be aware.

I transferred my profile pattern to a piece of scrap MDF so I could make a production pattern. The pattern has a flat area at one end to accommodate the top support plate that was attached to each leg in the last step.

Use this production pattern to trace nine copies onto ¾" plywood. Again, I used scraps for this as it would not be very visible. I rough cut the copies on the band saw (jig saw will work fine) to within ⅛" of the pencil line. Then, I stuck the production pattern to the copy with double-sided carpet tape and table-routed the copy down to final size, making an exact duplicate of the pattern. I then detached the pattern and repeated this step for the eight other copies. After all of the copies were cut out and routed to the same size, I glued them together in threes and screwed them together.

Shop Notes

Let the glue squeeze out dry for about an hour, then scrape it off. If you wait too long, it will be hard as a rock; if you do it too soon, you will have to work with liquid glue, which will be messy. Just rubbing it in is an option if you are painting, but if you are staining, you will wreck it. The glue will not accept stain the same as naked wood and you will see every glue splotch.

furnish

19

I set up a dado blade on my table saw to cut a groove to accommodate the support rods around the tire perimeter. I cut down the middle as best I could, but then I rotated the stack and cut again. Cutting in this way ensures a centered groove.

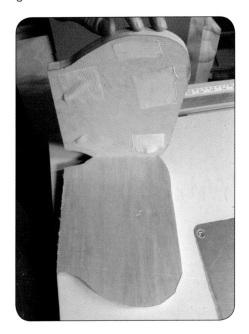

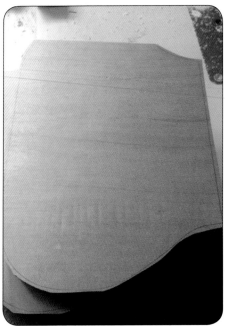

Step 6: Reunited

Now it is time to put the leg assemblies together. Remove the nut from one end of the support rod at the leg where you are working. Place the leg through the hole in the tire. Check to make sure the rubber is pressed flat against the top support plate and not in a bind against the leg (for appearance sake).

Place the leg support in place; it should fit snug in the tire, but not visibly deform it. I tapped the support into the proper position with a mallet to get it squared up with the "thirds" line and then twisted the leg to square it to the support. Repeat for all three legs.

Turn the whole thing over and drill a pilot hole through the tire's top support plate and into the leg support. Secure the tire, leg, and support together with appropriate length screws. Don't over-tighten the screws and mess up the tire. Although I used flat head screws, pan head screws would have probably been a better option . . . I just didn't have any long enough on hand.

furnish

and splintering off, thus preserving the quality of your table.

Step 7: Floored

Next, I cut a 17" diameter circle out of ½" scrap MDF for the bottom. I beveled the edges so it would fit the bead tightly. I then drilled through the bead and attached small plates with machine screws and washers to hold the bottom in place. I placed one support at each leg, then one support between each leg for a total of six supports.

The plates are leftover IKEA hardware. I filed and bent the outside end up a bit for a tight fit.

This is a good time to take a look at your legs . . . well, your table's legs, anyway. The bottom of each leg should have a slight ⅟₁₆" to ⅛" bevel sanded or planed onto them. The bevel serves two purposes. First, it makes the table look as if it is floating ever-so-slightly. Second, as the table is dragged around over the years, the bevel prevents the outside wood from catching the floor

Step 8: Tip Top

The only part of this project that isn't re-used or from my scrap pile is the top, and the only reason is because I had already used my decent plywood on other projects. You'll notice I have two circles on the plywood. That turned out to be way too heavy. I ended up using only one of the circles and saved the other for a future project.

Shop Notes:

To make working with sheet goods easier, it is a good idea to buy a $10 sheet of rigid foam insulation from a home center and keep it around just for a cutting surface. The foam provides stable support for your work piece all over its surface, and it is harmless to your blades. You can put it on your workbench if it is large enough, or in the driveway, etc. Then put the sheet on top and cut away. I use 1.5" foam because it provides plenty of room for error. Be sure you don't adjust the depth of your circular saw deeper than your foam or you will cut whatever is underneath.

After roughing out the circles to whatever diameter you want, it is time to make them nice rounds. I used a router with a circle trammel jig to cut the table top. There could be a multitude of Instructables on router technique, so I will just say: Don't bite off more than your router or you can chew.

Routers are very high speed tools (10,000–20,000 RPM). I use ½" bits these days, but when I started woodworking, I used ¼" bits. I have had two bits snap on me mid-cut and fly across the room. Metal flying across the room after being ejected by a 20,000 RPM machine will cause a pucker moment for sure. Wear safety equipment. Work safe. Read up on whatever process you use for circle cutting and be confident that you know what you are doing.

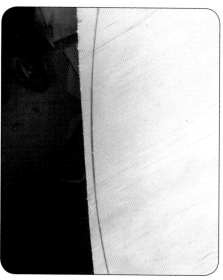

Step 9: Photo Finish

Although I like to build furniture, I don't have a tremendous amount of time to do so. As a result, we have some IKEA items hanging around. In our living room, we have the "Billy" bookcases in the dark (almost black) color. I really liked the color, and since they aren't going anywhere for a while, I opted to match this to their color as best I could.

Through trial and error—mostly error—I came up with a finishing process that worked well.

It is important to treat the surface of pretty much any soft or open-pored wood before staining, otherwise it will absorb the stain at an uneven rate. I knew this, and yet I continued on without doing it. As soon as I put stain to wood, I knew I had made a mistake. The softer rays of wood absorb the stain at a much greater rate than the harder rays. When you wipe the stain away, you end up with a zebra effect that will ruin a light finish. Luckily, I was going very dark, so I was able to fix my mistake.

Shop Notes:

There are several ways you can treat the wood to fix the uneven absorption problem. Commercially, there is "wood conditioner" that can be applied to the wood. It is convenient and dries quickly. I have heard of people making a wash of a wood glue/water mix as well, but I have never tried this. In the spirit of Instructables, I used a shop formula of three parts mineral spirits and one part satin polyurethane to fix my earlier jam.

Obviously, stir stains and polyurethane well before using and follow manufacturer recommendations (if you dare). When using polyurethane that has been hanging out in the shop for a while, it is always a pretty good idea to strain it through a cheese cloth after stirring, but before using it. I had some that was about eight months old and it was kind of nasty on top (see pictures). After straining, you are left with good working material that will give you much better results with fewer expletives.

Be careful with the dark stains not to sand through the stain. Due to the look I was going for, I opted to nix sanding and burnish the surface with 00 steel wool between coats to knock down any high spots. I use cut up shop rags for application also because I hate to see a good brush get ruined due to my hatred of cleaning them.

The stain mix I used was one part mineral spirits, one part polyurethane, and two parts "black onyx" stain. The addition of the poly seemed to prevent the solids in the stain from rubbing off so easily when I burnished between coats.

To emphasize a faux grain direction, I applied the stain in straight lines. I did not wipe the stain off because I wanted it to cover up the wild plywood grain pattern that was underneath. After the stain was completely dry, I applied two coats of polyurethane thinned down 3:1 poly to mineral spirits. Careful working with straight polyurethane . . . you may just end up with a honey-sticky mess on your hands. I personally don't use it unless it is thinned a bit.

Shop Notes:

I've never experienced it personally, but I don't want to. Spontaneous combustion: it's more than sci-fi. Many thinners, lacquers, stains, etc. have an exothermic reaction when they cure. If you ball up a soaked rag in an enclosed space, there is a very real danger of that exothermic reaction exceeding the flash point of the materials. Spread out your rags, clean them, or follow whatever procedures the manufacturer recommends so you don't blow yourself up or burn your own house down.

Step 10: Centering the Top and Wrap Up

To keep the top centered on the tire, you will need to put either a round attached to the underside, blocks, or something I haven't thought of. I used three blocks to keep the top centered on the tire table.

I had a hardwood cutoff about 1.5" × 1.5" × 7" in my scrap bin. I cut it into 2" pieces because that is the distance from the tire sidewall (bottom of the table top) to the inside of the bead.

Find the center of each block. Countersink a hole stopping short ¾" the other side, then drill through with a bit just bigger than the threads of the screw you are going to attach it with (#10 × 1.5" flat head wood screw in my case).

I made a jig out of scrap so I could trim the edges off the block to make a taper with my bandsaw. Otherwise, just sand it however you like. I then used a small block plane to get the profile I wanted and dressed it up with 100-grit and 220-grit sandpaper. I used a wipe on/wipe off technique with a mixture of 50/50 polyurethane and mineral spirits.

Shop Notes:

When you stain items with nooks and crannies, such as the screw hole on these blocks, or a box with a panel bottom for that matter, using an air compressor with a blower nozzle on the end is awesome for getting the excess polyurethane out of the cracks and grooves. This will keep you from getting as many runs and drips and will make for a neater presentation.

My top and the tire are almost the same diameter, so I measured the distance from the bead to the tread on the tire, then transferred that to the underside of the top. I had the "thirds" marked on the bottom side of the table top. In my case, I placed the outside edge of each finished block 6⅞" from the table top edge. Just a couple of tweaks and I had a tight fitting top.

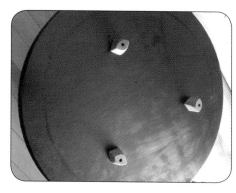

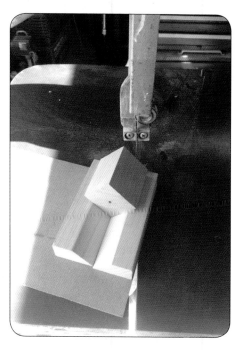

Concrete Lamp

By Ethan Lacy (hands_on)
(http://www.instructables.com/
id/concrete-lamp/)

This is a lamp made of concrete, glass, and steel.

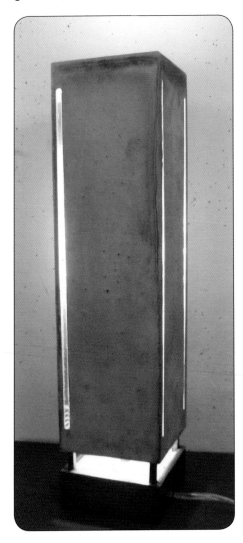

Step 1: Stuff You'll Need

- Concrete (Rockite works best) and something to mix it in/with

- Something to make formwork (Plywood or melamine work well. Foam Core can also be used.)
- 16" of 1.5" × ¼" steel bar stock
- 3 pieces of glass: ¼" thick: 12" × 4"; ⅛" thick: 12" × 3.5"; 1⁄16" thick: 12" × 3.5" (You can cut these yourself, or, easier yet, have a glass store cut them. They need to be fairly precise.)
- Screws, drill, drill bits, driver
- Foam core
- Glue gun
- Ceramic lamp socket
- 4" threaded lamp post
- Light bulb (bright)
- Lamp cord
- Lamp switch
- Screwdriver
- Space to make a mess
- Free time

Step 2: Making the Outer Formwork

First, you need to make the formwork. This will make or break (literally) this project. The more precise you can make it, the better. The inside volume needs to be exactly 4" square. You can use melamine, which will give a smooth surface. You can also use lumber or plywood, which can give the concrete texture. If you use ¾" material, you'll need two pieces 4" × 14", two at 5.5" × 14", and one for the bottom (which is actually the top) at 5.5" square. Again, make this as precise as possible. If you don't have access to a shop, you can use ½" foam core, a knife, and a ruler. Use a glue gun to glue it all together. If you coat the inside surface of the foam core with clear packing tape, the concrete won't stick, and you'll get a smooth, glassy surface on the concrete. The foam core method is probably easier and less forgiving, and works pretty much in the same way. Just make sure to seal the joints really well with the glue gun or packing tape. Otherwise, it will leak. Everywhere. The concrete will be very liquid-y. Like heavy cream. Don't underestimate its ability to find cracks and leak out of them.

Step 3: Make the Lamp Base

You can do this many different ways. I used steel filled with Rockite (concrete). This requires welding and grinding equipment. You can also just cast a hunk of concrete. Or, a block of wood. Just remember that you need to get the cord in there somehow. I used ¼" thick steel bar stock at 1.5" wide. To make a 4" square, you need two at 4" and two at 3.5". Weld these together and grind the welds. Then, because I'm going to pour concrete into the volume, I welded two little pieces of

¼" bar to keep the hunk of concrete from slipping out someday. Then drill a ¼" hole as far to the bottom as possible on one of the sides. This is for the cord.

We won't fill the bottom all the way with concrete, so that the cord can come out of the post and out our little hole. So put in a piece of foam core to the top level of the hole we just drilled. Seal the edges with the glue gun. We'll pour the concrete from the top. Then, with the glue gun, glue the threaded rod post onto the foam core. Make sure it's not off at an angle. The last two photos are what it looks like when it's dry, top and bottom. Get the idea? I think the next time I do this, I'll probably forget about floating it above the base. I think a hunk of wood could look nice. This took too long.

Now for our first pour. This will be good practice for the big one. I recommend getting Rockite. It's available at a lot of smaller hardware stores. The stuff is awesome. It's like plaster, just a lot stronger, and it has a beautiful smooth finish. Mix it as per the instructions so that it's like heavy cream. Or melted ice cream. Not too runny! The more water, the weaker. It's easy to add too much water. Add it slowly.

Pour it in just short of the top of the steel base. Now, this is the annoying part. I don't think I would do this again this way, but here goes. I wanted the thing to "float" off the base a bit. So I decided to cast in some ¼" steel bar legs. I welded these little bits of wire on to the legs so that it would adhere well to the concrete. I won't get into the details, because I think it's a bit of a cockamamied way to do this. But you need to make sure the wire won't interfere with the glass for the main pour.

For this step, I'm just setting them into the base about ¼", so that the shade will sit securely into the base. These will be easy to remove once it's hard, and then I'll cast the legs into the shade. I know, ridiculous. The trick is you have to somehow hold these little guys in position while the concrete dries. This can be accomplished with small clamps. Or maybe duct tape. But have a game plan before you pour. I didn't have one, so this is my improvised, half-assed on-the-spot effort. It worked, mainly because Rockite dries fast. It will start to set up in about fifteen minutes. After an hour, you can carve it with a blade. In twenty-four hours, it's wicked hard, but you can sand it and shape it a bit. After a week it's rock solid.

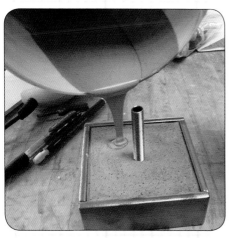

Step 4: Preparing the Mold

You'll need to build some formwork for the void in the middle. I used foam core and melamine. I think it would be better to use all foam core, or a solid piece of rigid insulation foam (usually pink or blue, available at Home Depot). The reason for this is because you have to get it out once the concrete dries. I thought the foam core would be squishable enough. But it was a pain to get it out. So, use foam, and you can coat it in packing tape for a better finish and easier release. Regardless, it needs to be 3" square, exactly, and the same length as the outer mold, *plus* the amount you want it to "float" above the base, if you want to do that. I used ¾". This way, the base can rest on this while we cast the feet into the shade, and it'll keep the right spacing (see photos).

31

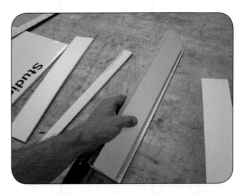

You can glue the glass directly to the inner formwork, as shown. This way, the glass will be exposed on the inside of the shade. This glue will come off easily when you release it. The thick piece of glass overhangs ½″ on either side of the inner formwork. The other two pieces butt into it and overhang ½″ on their respective sides. Obviously, you can modify this layout. There should be at least ¾″ on the top and bottom. This is critical so that the concrete has some structure, since we're cutting it all up with the glass. Now slide it into the outer formwork. This might require loosening some screws. This is not an easy step. You'll have to futz with it. If your measurements were good, it will be easier.

It's critical that the glass butts into the outer formwork, exposing the edge and ensuring that it is securely glued to the inner formwork, as well as exposing the inside so the light can get out. This will take patience. Trial, error, adjust. The last step: Once the formwork is adjusted, tight, and sealed (you can use the glue gun like caulk if need be), invert the base over the top so that you can cast the legs into the shade. Make sure they're reasonably straight and that everything looks good. Take it out.

furnish

Step 5: The Big Pour

Mix up enough Rockite. I'll leave this up to you to figure out. Pour it slowly into the mold, until it comes flush with the top edge. You can overfill it a bit and then scrape it flush after about ten minutes. Invert the base over it to cast in the legs. You can glue these temporarily into the base with a glue gun or use duct tape or something. You don't want to lose them to the concrete abyss. Once it all looks good, put it away for at least twelve hours.

Step 6: Break the Mold

Take off the base, but leave the sides attached. It's tempting to look, but it'll be easier and safer to ream out the middle if you leave the sides attached. If you used solid foam, get a big, fat, long drill bit and ream it out as much as possible. Stick screwdrivers in there, putty knives, whatever you need to do to get that foam out. Foam core is the same deal. Needle-nose pliers and yanking might help. This step is a pain in the ass. Take your time and be gentle. It's possible to break this thing.

After you get the center pretty well cleaned out, you can take the outer mold off. Make sure it didn't crack anywhere. (If it did, you can fix cracks with superglue.) You might need to excavate the glass edges a bit so they are exposed. Be gentle. You can use a flat edge screwdriver to do this. You might also need to do this on the inside if some of the Rockite got in between the formwork and the glass. It should chip off. Be gentle. Finally, you can lightly sand the sharp corners and rinse the whole thing off in the sink. Make sure all the glass is exposed cleanly inside and out. If it came out on the first try, nice work. If not, hopefully you can re-use the glass and re-pour.

furnish

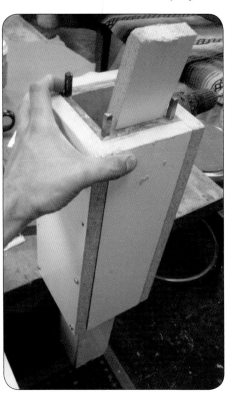

Step 7: Assemble Lamp

Put the lamp together. Thread the cord up through the base holes and screw the thing on top. You can put a switch on the cord too, if you want. I'm not getting into wiring here. If you don't know what you're doing, ask someone who does.

Use a bright bulb. I used fluorescent (incandescents will get the thing really hot—better to use compact fluorescents and less energy at the same time). This bulb is a 150 watt equivalent, which uses 32 watts. The shade will block a lot of the light. Notice that you can see through the shade on the thick piece of glass. (Even when switched off!)

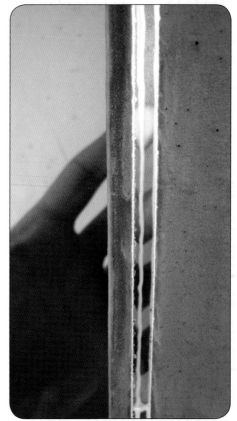

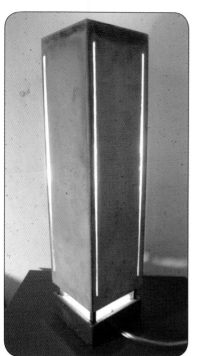

Road Sign Coffee Table

By William Holman (wholman)
(http://www.instructables.com/
id/Road-Sign-Coffee-Table/)

Road signs are a great material—strong, durable, weatherproof, and graphically interesting. I made this table out of two old signs; the legs came out of a sign that was 1' × 7', and the top was made from a sign that was 2' × 5'. Each is about thirty years old, which made the aluminum kind of brittle and prone to cracking on the bends. Basically, I drilled holes in the sign to weaken it, then hit it with a hammer while holding it against an edge to effect the folds. Again, because these signs were quite old, and not in the best condition, some cracking and breaking occurred. I also was pushing the bending radius and tightness of the folds, which obviously was pushing it a bit too far in some cases.

Lastly, these older signs are considerably thicker than newer ones, which I suspect also contributed to the deterioration of the seams. However, I still think the Instructable is valuable, in that this table is an experiment that enabled me to learn a lot about the material and the aesthetic possibilities of road signs.

I got the signs for free from some friends who inherited them with their apartment; other possible sources are junkyards, recycling centers, and eBay. Don't steal signs. Road signs are in place to protect people on the road; removing them illegally could have serious consequences, whether or not you get caught.

Since the signs were free, the only costs were drill bits and #8 machine bolts. I estimate the whole project was $10–$15. However, this method is pretty time consuming. Fortunately, it is the sort of thing that can be broken up over a series of weekends or nights. I took me a month of working in my spare time to make it—roughly twenty-five hours. Dimensions are all approximate, as I understand you may be trying to replicate this with different-dimensioned signs. The important thing to keep in mind is the overall ergonomics and human scale; a coffee table should sit no more than 17"–18" off the ground, and be at least 18" wide by whatever length the couch is.

Step 1: Model

I made some study models out of Bristol board to figure out my strategy. The photos are fairly self-explanatory as to the process. Making simple models to scale is a great way to think in 3D and figure out exactly how something might look and feel. The finished table does not strictly conform to this model, but it is very close. Use the dimensions of your sign and some cereal-box cardboard to come up with variations on folding strategies, leg configurations, and attachment schemes. Make several models, put them next to one another, and choose the one that looks the best and uses the available material most efficiently.

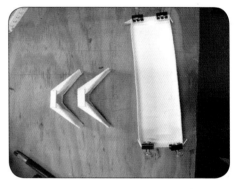

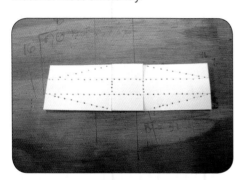

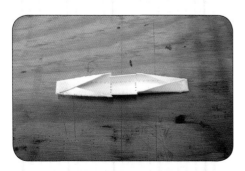

furnish

furnish

Step 2: Legs!

The legs are easier to make than they appear. Using an overall rectangle 12" × 18", two straight lines and two diagonal lines become folds; these folds eventually overlap one another to make a tapering form that can be pinned together with two machine bolts. The geometry is straightforward: Divide the piece lengthwise into three 4" × 18" strips. Run diagonals from two outside corners to the two middle lines. I laid it out in chalk; you can draw on the back with a Sharpie as well. Use a ⅛" drill bit to put pilot holes on one inch centers. Go back and drill every other one with a ¼" bit; get the alternating ones with a ⅜" bit. To bend, screw the sign down to a piece of wood through the smaller diameter holes, and hit with a mallet or small sledgehammer to achieve the bends. Once the two "wings" overlap, hammer them flat and clamp them together. Drill through with a ³⁄₁₆" drill bit and pin the metal together with #8 or #10 machine bolts and washers.

As you can see, these legs are asking a lot of the material. All four of them had at least some minor cracking. This can be avoided with newer, thinner signs; this table would also turn out quite well if executed in thinner sheet steel, as it isn't as tough to bend. Be careful not to cut yourself on the sharp edges of the aluminum; the shavings from the drilling make for nasty little splinters that are hard to see, hard to get out, and hurt a lot.

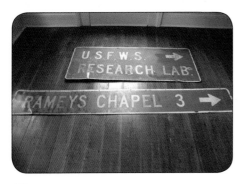

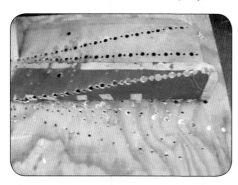

it was 90°. If the curb by your house is chamfered at an oblique angle, bend it as far as you can with that curb, then lay it down flat with the edges curled up. Lay a 2" × 4" along the seam and stand on that, then swing the mallet towards your legs to bend the sides upward. Clamp a block to the corners and curl the triangular flap in at each corner. The joinery and folding of the top is basically like wrapping a Christmas present.

As you can see in the photos, the two short end pieces broke off from the stress of the bends. One of the main reasons for that is the lever arm of the bend is only 3"; if the rim of the table was 10" or 12", there would be enough material to act as effective lever and peel up the bend. If they had stayed attached, the table would stronger and more stable. However, it is not a strict requirement that they be attached. The table is plenty strong with them being additive pieces; that said, try to avoid them breaking off if possible. As I said in the introduction, this is an experiment, and it is up to you to improve and expand this basic process.

Step 3: Toppin'

The top is a 2' × 5' sign. On its own, this piece of metal was quite floppy. To stiffen it up and give two edges to bolt through, fold down a three-inch border on all four sides. Mark your lines, and then drill the holes in the same alternating pattern of diameters as you did for the legs. Make a slit with a hacksaw or an angle grinder in each corner, running at 45° from the outside corner to the intersection of the lines of holes. To bend, I put the line of holes on the edge of a curb and stood on the sign, then beat it with the hammer until

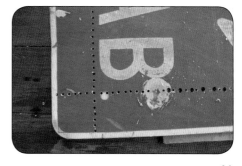

Step 4: Assembly

Now that you have a top and some legs, all that's left is to put them all together. It's pretty straightforward; three bolts go through the short side of the top into the side of the legs and two bolts go on the long side. Each bolt does double duty, securing the legs to the body of the table as well as securing the corner bends of the top to itself. Measure out a slope on the side pieces and mark with a Sharpie. Clamp in place, drill through, and tighten up. Run a level (or in this case, a 2″ × 4″ with a tiny combo square, because I don't have a long level) across the bottom of the legs to make sure the thing will sit flat when you're done. Repeat for all four legs. Flip it over and straight chill.

road sign coffee table

Reclaimed Bowling Lane Table

By hoda0013
(http://www.instructables.com/
id/Bowling-Lane-Table/)

I recently moved into my first house and was in need of a dining room table. I saw a picture of a table that used an old section of bowling lane for its top and decided that I'd like to build something similar for myself. With about thirty hours of work over a few months, I was able to turn a tattered piece of wood into a beautiful, sturdy table that should never need replacement.

To find the lane section, I did a Craigslist search for bowling lanes and happened to find a guy about fifty miles away from me that was selling lane sections that he procured during a demolition job he was hired for. I paid about $300 for an 8' section with the arrow inlays. The section was about 2.5" thick and weighed about 250 pounds.

Step 1: Preparing the Lane

The first step in the process was to add support to the lane section to keep it from sagging. When the lanes are installed in the bowling alley, they are built in place. The builders lay down long strips of maple and side nail them to the adjacent maple pieces. No glue is used in the entire process, which means that, once the lane is taken up from the floor, it doesn't behave like a single slab of wood. All of the maple pieces are still tied together via the nails, but there is a certain amount of flex that the lane has. If not supported properly, the lane will sag quite dramatically in the middle due to its weight. To add support to the lane, I chose to inlay aluminum bars width-wise across the bottom of the table.

Using a hand router and a piece of metal to serve as a guide, I routed out three pockets across the width of the table. I made the pockets ¾" wide to accommodate the ⅝" aluminum square stock, and I made sure to make them a little deeper than necessary, because I needed to sand the bottom down and didn't want the belt of the sander to touch the metal pieces.

With the pockets routed, I set out drilling the aluminum bar stock. I spaced the holes so that each was centered with a piece of maple. The goal was to tie all of the pieces of maple together using the bar so that the table wouldn't sag in the future. When this was done, I ran screws through each hole and into the bottom of the table.

This resulted is a sturdy top that shouldn't sag.

top and bottom surfaces. Because the aluminum inlays on the bottom side were recessed, we were able to totally flatten that side out. If I hadn't recessed them, the shop said that they wouldn't have been able to sand that side. I felt that this was a great deal, because not only did the sanding come out perfect, but it saved me countless hours trying to recreate that process at home. I still had a little bit of hand sanding to do on the edges, but that was relatively easy compared to the top and bottom. I worked up to 220-grit sandpaper and called it good.

The lane was then ready for a few coats of polyurethane to seal it up. I used an oil-based polyurethane with a satin finish made by Minwax for the finish because I wanted to keep the natural color of the wood. I applied first to the bottom and sides of the lane, then I flipped it and did the top half. I applied about six coats in all, sanding with 220-grit sandpaper between each coat. The finish went on beautifully and I was really happy with the results.

Step 2: Sanding and Finishing the Lane

When I picked up the lane section from the seller, it was in pretty good shape, though the top was dirty and covered in decades of bowling alley oil, dirt, etc. I really wanted to sand a layer off the top to help clean it and a layer off the bottom to create a nice flat surface to mount legs to. I struggled with trying to decide the best way to sand the lane down and finally came across a local wood working shop that had a wide enough Timesaver belt sander. I brought the lane in on my day off and paid $60 to have them sand about ⅛" off of the

Step 3: Making the Legs

Because I don't really have a wood shop at home, I decided to have the legs CNC routed from 18mm-thick Baltic Birch plywood. This way all I had to do was glue the various sections together to make thicker sections, sand, and apply a finish, not to mention the neat tricks you can do with this type of manufacturing process, such as using slots as passages for bolts, creating pockets to keep weight down, and having overall accuracy, that make it possible to do things that would be more difficult using traditional woodworking methods.

I designed the legs using Solidworks and sent the files to a local CNC routing shop called RoboCut CNC. A few days later, I had the parts in hand and was ready to start gluing them together. I was amazed at how well the Baltic Birch cut. There wasn't any chipout on the edges and everything fit together perfectly.

To glue the parts together, I spread Titebond II wood glue on the faces to be glued and pressed them together using about eight C-clamps per part. Because alignment was critical, I included holes and pockets in all of the sections to accept two dowel pins. The dowels serve to align the sections together. This is important for looks, but also because I had several through holes that would need to accept hardware and, if those were misaligned, the hardware wouldn't fit correctly and could create an unsightly gap between the hardware and the wood.

The gluing went well, but there are some things I'd do differently next time. When pressure from the clamps is applied, some excess glue will squish out at the edges. My instinct was to wipe the glue off with a wet paper towel. Although this cleaned the bulk of the glue off, it also pressed a thin layer of glue into the pores on the edge of the wood. This created an ugly yellow glue smear that needed a lot of sanding time

to remove. Next time I would just let the glue be until it was dry and then remove it with a sharp chisel. This would have saved me lots of sanding time. Oh well.

With the legs glued together, it was time to apply a finish to them. By this time, it is really cold where I live, so applying finish in my unheated garage wasn't an option. Because of this, I needed to do the work in my basement, which meant that odor from the finish was a major concern. To cut down on the amount of VOCs in the air, I opted for a water-based polyurethane finish made by Minwax. The odor was almost nonexistent and I was happy with the results.

Step 4: Machining the Hardware

The table legs are built in several sections, which are then bolted together to form "trestle style" legs. To attach the sections together, I used cross dowels that I custom machined. They are made from 1.25" diameter aluminum round stock and there are twenty of them in total. These were part of a simple procedure that involved facing each piece to the right length (about 4.4"), putting a small chamfer on the edges using a file, slightly turning down the diameter to fit in the hole properly, and then drilling a tapping into a ⅜", 16 thread hole through the middle.

I had designed the holes in the wooden pieces to be slightly oversized by about 0.005"; however, I learned that the tolerance on the aluminum stock was slightly larger than expected so the aluminum stock would not fit in the holes as is. The benefit of this ended up being that I could get the fit of the hardware just right and that turning down the diameter left a nicer finish on the part.

Also, because of the gluing step for the wood, there was a little bit of glue residue left on the inside of the holes that the cross dowels needed to slide into. I hadn't counted on that and needed to get the glue out of there. To do this, I turned a tool on the lathe that was simply a long round piece of aluminum that had a diameter just slightly less than the diameter of the hole in the wood. I centered this in the hole and, with a few blows of the hammer, the tool was forced through the hole and sheared off any glue that was in there. The cross dowels were then machined slightly smaller in diameter than the tool; and, when slipped into place, everything fit perfectly.

Step 5: Assembly

This was the fun and easy part. Using the cross dowels and ⅜", 16 thread × 5" bolts (available at Home Depot) and some washers, I attached each section together until the table legs were standing. I also added some felt pads to the bottom of the table. It was pretty easy to do this by first assembling the legs and leg cross bars, and then adding the two long spanner pieces last. I had the table top resting on sawhorses that were slightly taller than the leg assembly. I slid the sawhorses to the extreme ends of the table top and was able to just slide the leg assembly underneath; then, I removed the sawhorses one by one so that the top was resting on the legs. Using some long screws, I was able to attach the top to the legs in a semi permanent way so that everything will break down easily for moving someday.

Section 2

Decorate

This is how to make an excellent excuse for driving a lag bolt into your wall: the Concrete Light Bulb Wall Hook. Functional, yet stylish, it gives a nice industrial design feel wherever you mount it.

Last winter, after breaking out the serious cold weather gear, I found myself fighting the coat rack next to the front door. It was, to put it bluntly, failing miserably. Tipping over, breaking off, it was a mess. I swore before the next winter I would drive some serious hooks into the wall that would handle all my heavy overcoat needs. I just hadn't seen any kickass hooks that I liked enough to justify making serious holes in my walls.

Cut to the last few months. I've been playing around, trying to make a concrete lightbulb. Why? Because I find the contrast of blending a new material like concrete in an everyday shape like a lightbulb to be a great design element. So while messing around with these guys, I realized this would be a great excuse to drive lag bolts into my wall for hooks. By embedding a lag bolt into the concrete lightbulb, I could make a wall hook that was useful enough to handle anything I wanted to hang off it. Thus this project was born.

Step 1: Tools and Materials

You will need a work area where a little sand and concrete mix or glass shards is not an issue. Make sure you have a small brush and dustpan available at all times. Normally you wait till the end to shatter the light bulb, but it can happen at any point in this process. So be ready for cleanup from the very start.

Tools

- Small pair of pliers
- Small pair of wire cutters
- Small screwdriver
- Carbide scribe. You can use something like an awl or even a long skinny nail, but I found my trusty old scribe to be invaluable in this.
- Plastic tub to mix the concrete in. I used an empty 5-pound tub of spreadable margarine.
- A scrap of wood to mix the concrete with. You could use an old wooden spoon or something like that if needed.
- Plastic spoon to put the concrete mix into the light bulb
- A measuring cup and measuring spoons for adding the correct amount of concrete mix and water
- A toothbrush you won't be using for your teeth anymore
- Coffee stirrer and plastic cups you "borrowed" from Starbucks
- Gloves and safety glasses. A must because the glass bulb often breaks and little shards go flying in all directions, including straight at your eyes.
- Miscellaneous items like Sharpies, some rags, etc.

Materials

Concrete is a mix of cement, water, and aggregates. My research showed that a sand mix, aka mortar mix, is good when using a smooth surfaced mold like the inside of a light bulb. It gives a very high shine when cured. A sand mix is different from your generic concrete in that the aggregates don't have any gravel, just various sizes of sand. I decided to do it with mortar mix instead of your standard bag of generic concrete.

- Quikrete Mortar mix. I got the 10-pound bag at the local home improvement store for $2. This is enough to do over a dozen light bulbs. I could have purchased the 60-pound bag for $7 at a much lower cost/volume, but this project really doesn't need that much.
- Light bulbs. Just the cheapest standard sized incandescent light bulbs you can find. I got a pack of four at Wal-Mart for $0.77. Can't beat that with a stick.
- Water. You'll need about 4 tablespoons worth. I kept a bottle of water nearby on the bench and refilled it from the tap when needed.
- Lag Bolt. I'm using a $5/16"$ lag bolt, 3.5" long. Without cutting off the head, $5/16"$ was the largest sized lag bolt I could fit into the light bulb. I didn't want to cut off the head because the head gives the bolt a lot of grip when embedded in the concrete. With a lag bolt $5/16"$ in diameter, I can drill in the wall a $1/4"$ hole to get a good balance between grip and ease of installing. In other words, it turns easily into the wall yet holds really well.

Step 2: Hollow Out the Light Bulb

In the beginning, I found the directions at TeamDroid to be a great help on how to do this. Now that I've done it over a dozen times it's routine. With practice this becomes quick and simple. A lot of the time, you are poking around inside the light bulb trying to break off the internal glass bits. Do this over a trashcan and frequently shake the light bulb out over the trashcan to get rid of the glass shards. Wear safety glasses at all times. More than once some glass flew up towards my face when I was doing this.

First, with a blob of solder in the middle, grip the metal circle at the bottom of the light bulb with your pliers and gently pry it up from the dark purple glass insulator. This is pulling a wire in the middle that you want to break, so just pull it off. Once that is done, take your carbide scribe and, over a trash can, pry into the hole you just made in the purple glass insulator and break up that purple glass. You want to remove the entire purple glass insulator from the light bulb body. I use the scribe to start some cracks and lift off a section of it, then I followed up with the screwdriver to get the rest. Turn the light bulb upside down and shake out all the glass bits that have fallen inside. Inside there is a small glass tube that pokes up into the glass insulator. You may or may not have already broken that off by now. If not, just lever the screwdriver against it until it snaps loose. Empty it into the trashcan.

Now you have a hole in the bottom of the light bulb. At this point I take my pliers and gently bend over the metal tabs on the inside of the hole so there is no "lip" on the inside. Later, when you have broken up the rest of the inside pieces, there isn't anywhere for the bits to catch and stay in the light bulb when you shake it out.

There should be a wire visible inside that's soldered to the side of the metal screw piece. Take your wire cutters and cut the wire as close to the side of the bulb as possible. Now, the inside has a glass cylinder you need to break off; clean up the edges to finish the job. Take your scribe or screwdriver and put it down into the light bulb until it meets resistance. Tap it gently until something breaks. Then, using the screwdriver, lever against the side of the light bulb to clean out whatever remaining glass bits are left. You want the neck of the light bulb to be clear from the hole all the way down the body. Turn the bulb over and shake it out one more time to get rid of the last of the internal glass pieces floating loose.

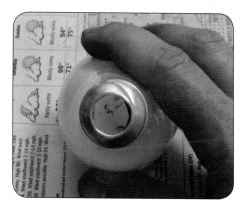

Take a toothbrush and, while dry, push it into the light bulb and start loosening up the dry white powder. Especially in the neck of the bulb. Don't worry if you can't get the stuff the toothbrush can't reach at this point. I found the bulb cleans out easier if you loosen up the white powder in the neck before it gets wet. Now take it over to the sink and add a little soap and water. Scrub around with the toothbrush and shake the bulb to get the water everywhere. Pull out the toothbrush and then wash out the soapy water from the bulb. At this point, it's all nice and clean inside without any soapy residue. Set it aside to dry out. Now it's time to mix up the concrete.

decorate

Step 3: Mix Up the Concrete

This is the part that's more art than science. I've found that in the small batches this project calls for, it's very easy to add too much or too little water to the mix. When you are mixing an entire 60-pound bag of concrete, being off a teaspoon on the water doesn't matter that much. When you are mixing up just a cup of concrete, that teaspoon starts to matter.

Mortar mix, when cured in a glass mold like we are using, gives a very nice glossy surface. The lower the amount of water you use, the smoother the surface is and the stronger the resulting cured concrete is. However, the lower the amount of water you use, the harder it is to have it fill in the gaps on the sides and it leaves lots of holes and divots. One of the main issues of the water to cement ration is getting the mix liquid-like enough to spread out but not too liquid-like that it loses its strength. Finding the correct compromise between these two issues is really a matter of practice and personal taste. I would suggest you play around with it in multiple bulbs if you are interested in getting the best result you can. The ratio I've found works well is about 1.25 cups of the mortar mix and a hair under 4 tablespoons of water. So measure out a little less than 4 tablespoons of water and put that into your plastic tub. This is more mortar mix than you need to fill a light bulb, but there is always some spillage, and trying

to reduce the amount means even more accuracy on the water measurement. This is a good place to start.

Slowly mix in the mortar mix a little at a time. Let a little bit get wet, then a little more, then a little more while stirring the whole thing. It's a bit like making biscuit dough at this level, but you're pouring the dry into the wet instead of the other way around. The consistency should be good enough that the mortar mix wants to stick together in one large clump, but it isn't sopping wet. If you feel you need to add more water or mortar mix to get it correct, then go for it. Just do it a little bit at a time. A small amount of either material makes a large impact at this point.

Once it's at a consistency you like, keep stirring nice and slow for a few minutes. You want everything to be thoroughly wetted as much as possible. **Note:** At this moment the clock starts and you have thirty to forty-five minutes to finish the light bulb before the mortar mix starts to harden up. Once you have thoroughly mixed up the mortar mix, bring out the light bulb and start filling it up.

Step 4: Start Filling Up the Light Bulb with the Mortar Mix

You are working on a time limit at this point as the mortar mix starts to set. If you can get it all done in thirty minutes or so, it should be fine. Put your light bulb into a small plastic tub with the hole pointing upwards. When you are adding the mix there is always spillage and you don't want that all over your work area. I put a little bit of sand in the bottom so it will stay straight to begin with; once you add a few spoonfuls of the mortar mix, it stands up straight on its own. Take a plastic spoon and scoop up a level amount of the wet mortar mix. Holding the end of the spoon over the hole in the light bulb, use your finger on the other hand to push it down into the hole. Some will spill over the edges of the hole—that's okay. You made almost twice the volume of mortar mix that will go into the light bulb.

After four or five spoonfuls into the light bulb, you want to vibrate it so the mortar mix liquefies and spreads out evenly on the inside. Shake it back and forth to make it liquefy. If there is an air bubble visible on the side that just won't fill in no matter how much you shake, tap it repeatedly with your fingertip. This moves the bubble up and the liquid towards the tapping. Do these steps, a handful of scoops, and then much shaking and taping to fill in the gaps and make it all liquid like until you reach half way up the neck of the bulb. At that point, it's time to add the lag bolt.

Step 5: Put in the Lag Bolt and Finish Adding the Mortar Mix

Before putting in the lag bolt, mark off with a Sharpie where 1.5" is from the pointy end so you know how far to push it down. Put the lag bolt into the mortar mix. Because the light bulb shape has some undercutting with the mold, the mortar mix wants to clump up in the middle of the bulb and not grip the sides. You can use the head of the lag bolt to tap down the pile in the middle of the bulb so it starts filling in all the gaps. Keep adding mortar mix around the lag bolt to fill it up. Holding the lag bolt firmly to make sure it does not rattle, keep shaking the bulb and tapping the sides to fill in gaps and liquefy the mortar mix. Take the coffee stirrer you "borrowed" from Starbucks and use that to tap down the mortar mix. You want to keep adding the mix, tamp and fill, tamp and fill. Finally the entire bulb is all done and you are tamping on the top. You want the mortar mix to be level with the top of the hole but not sticking out in a bulge. When you are all done, put the light bulb with the lag bolt pointing up in a spare plastic cup. The ones I used were also borrowed from Starbucks. Take a rag and clean up the metal threaded part of the light bulb as well as you can—you don't want the mortar mix drying on it. Set this to the side for at least seventy-two hours to let the mortar mix cure. I normally write the date it was made on the glass with a Sharpie so I can keep track.

Step 6: Crack the Light Bulb

Let the mortar mix cure for at least seventy-two hours. A few days more is a better. When the mortar is cured, you will break the light bulb into little bits and pieces. Glass will be flying in all directions, so wear safety glasses and at least one glove (like in the pictures) at all times! Over a trash can, hold the bulb in one hand that has a glove on it. I've tried to use gloves on both hands at this stage and didn't have the fine control I wanted. You might be able to do it.

With a hard metal object, start striking the side of the light bulb. I'm using my carbide scribe. The glass will start to crack and form spider web fractures. Keep hitting. Eventually small pieces will fall and/or fly off of the bulb. When you have formed a good number of cracks around the bulb, take a toothbrush and scrub it vigorously over the entire bulb. This will brush any glass grit or loose pieces into the trashcan. Then take your carbide scribe (or awl or sharp nail) and start to pry up the edges of the glass left on the bulb. Some of it will come off in large chunks, some of it will come off a little at a time. Try to aim for the trashcan but know that it won't all go in there; some of it will pop up and go in any direction. If a large piece of glass doesn't want to come up and doesn't have any cracks in it, beat it with the metal object some more to create the spider web. Every so often, take the toothbrush and rub down the light bulb to get rid of any ground in glass or loose bits.

When all the glass has been removed from the light bulb, take your scribe and carefully go around the neck of the bulb where the metal met the glass. Make sure there are no loose glass shards under the lip of the metal. Shake and tap the bulb to see what floats loose. When you are done, take a shop brush and run it over the entire bulb one more time to

decorate

get any glass grit or loose pieces out of the holes in the concrete.

It's done! The mortar mix often leaves pits and holes even with all that shaking and tapping you did, but I think it adds a bit of character to the whole thing and makes each one you do unique. Feel the glossy smooth glass finish on the bulb and how it reflects the light. Now it's time to mount it!

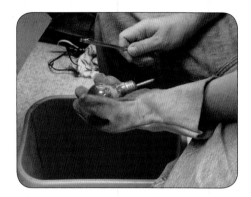

Step 7: Mount It On the Wall

Now that you have this killer Concrete Light Bulb Wall Hook, it's time to mount it into the wall. The instructions here are fairly simple. Find the stud. This wants a wood stud in the wall. There are multiple ways to find a wood stud; I'm using a cheapie stud finder. Now, drill the hole. Using a ¼" drill bit, drill a hole 1.5" deep into the wall, then screw it in. The hole is big enough that you can screw it in, but the bite is good enough that it can hold just about anything you want to hang off it. Heavy overcoats, small children, whatever strikes your fancy. Hang your hat. Or you could use it as a hat hook.

decorate

decorate

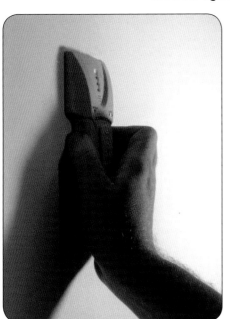

This is a handmade tea light holder, crafted from a log. I shaped a log from our firewood pile into a slab and drilled holes for the tea lights. It's pretty simple really, but the most important part is picking an attractive piece of wood and paying attention to nice finishing.

Tools

- A log shaping tool (band saw, hand saw, chainsaw, hatchet, plane, belt sander, mill, your teeth etc.)
- A large Forstner bit (either 1.5" or 1⅝")
- Drill
- Bike (optional)

Disclaimer: Use common sense or succumb to evolution.

on either side. It should be long enough for 1 to 100 candles, but I think odd numbers of candles looks best. I made two: one from option one and another from option three.

Option One: Take some firewood from your woodpile. Make sure it isn't rotten and that it doesn't have woodworm or other defects (unless you think they may look good).

Option Two: Go to a lumber yard or equivalent and tell them what you're trying to make; they can probably give you a scrap for very little or free.

Option Three: I met a tree surgeon who was working on a street near my house. I asked him for a fresh log that was in the back of his truck. I had to call him a number of times as he was an old guy who seemed to be hard of hearing—don't give up! He gave me a maple log for $2. Now, this is where the bike comes in. I was riding home when I met him, so I carried the log home bungee corded to my bike. Be careful, as it's impossible to steer and you become a very nice projectile.

Step 1: Acquiring Materials

For the wood, you have a couple of different options, but in general you want a hard wood (i.e., not pine 2" × 4") with nice grain and points of interest, like a knot or a rough edge with some bark. It can be any shape or size you like, as long as it is wide and deep enough to fit a tea light with a little extra space

Step 2: Shaping

Take a look at your piece of wood and search for your candle holder within the log. I kept one edge close to the edge of the log for bark and picked a length where there was a knot. To blank it out, you need one of the shapers mentioned earlier. I would suggest a saw, but I had a go with the hatchet for my firewood log attempt, which left the final piece more rustic, as there were deeper gouges from the hatchet. As you can see from the pictures, I made a cuboid, but you could make it any shape you like. Once you have the basic shape done, you can work on it with progressively finer tools—like a plane, then sander, then finer sandpaper. You should try using a plane if you haven't already—they are really fun, and they make a big mess of wood curls everywhere. A belt sander is really helpful, but not necessary. I put mine upside down in the vise so I could bring the work to the tool, not the other way round, which is easier for smaller stuff.

Step 3: Snack and Touchups

First things first, get something to eat, like a cup of tea and a cinnamon bun.

Look for any problem areas—where bark is lifting up, really big gouges, etc. For bark that's lifting up, fix it right away, because, when the break is fresh, the fibers connect back together better. Get some carpenter's glue and squidge it into the crack with your finger or a scrap piece of wood. Put a clamp on it and leave it to dry. If you made a big gouge, either make it part of the rustic look or fill it with wood filler. Follow the directions on the packet. Now you'll need to do more sanding to get rid of excess glue/filler. Doing lots of sanding with finer and finer grits is really worth it. Notice I'm sanding before drilling. The Forstner bits make a really clean cut into the piece, so it's easier to sand before you have holes to negotiate.

Step 4: Drilling Holes

Decide how many candles you want. For any odd number of candles, measure to the middle and place a mark; this is where you will drill for the middle candle. The rest of the marks are a little harder to explain, but you want an equal distance between the edges of your candles, not between centers, so you will need to know the radius of your drill bit. Then draw it around your drill mark with a compass.

Now you can measure from the edge. Position the remaining candles equal distances apart, and mark for holes. Or make a jig from scrap material, like I used for the firewood piece. First, drill a hole in a board for the jig, then move the edge of your jig to the edge of where you just drilled, and drill a hole through the hole in the jig. Keep moving it up, then cut off the end when you can't make any more holes. The most expensive part of this project was the Forstner bit, at around $30, but it's worth it to buy a quality tool. You can make lots more candle holders. I even have a few other projects that use the same bit. I found that a 1.5" Forstner bit was the largest Home Depot sells, but this only fits the tea light without the cup. If you want to fit the cup (which I suggest, so you don't set fire to the candle holder or have a waxy mess to scrape out), you will need a bigger size, which I found at an old school hardware store, Preston Hardware in Ottawa. They gave me a 1⅝", which fits the cup.

Note: All tea lights are not created equal. Mine are from IKEA. I found some others that are smaller and may fit into a 1.5" hole. Check what candles you have or can get before you buy a bit. If you have a drill press, this will be much easier. You can set the depth stop for the size of a candle. Then just start making wood chips. A hand drill would work okay, but clamp your piece securely and make sure you drill straight.

Step 5: Finish Up

If the edges of the holes are rough, give them a little sanding. Think about finishes—there are many you could do. My favorite is tung oil, which I used on the chopping board. I left the maple candle holder natural. I treated the longer log holder with liming wax, which brings out the grain in a big way. You could also stain it. Be careful about using potentially flammable finishes.

Buy some nice candles. I got beeswax tea lights from an environmental/organic shop called Arbour in Ottawa. They smell great. Wrap it up, and give someone a piece of firewood instead of a lump of coal. Now you've bought the expensive bit, make a few more or have a go at making a chopping board.

Simple Branching Coat Rack

By Sly Lee (slylee)
(http://www.instructables.com/
id/Simple-Branching-Coat-
Rack/)

This rack was inspired by a design I saw on Etsy. I do like to support local artists and craftsmen when possible, but at $75, this was not an option for me at the moment. In addition, I had a couple of extra branches and wood lying around. And, of course, as always, if it can be built, I will build it.

I have been teaching my girlfriend how to do basic handiwork, and for this project, I largely instructed and supervised while she assembled it. She did most of the sawing, nailing, and assembling.

- Saw
- Handsaw for cutting the branches
- Table saw, miter saw, chop saw, or handsaw to cut the frame

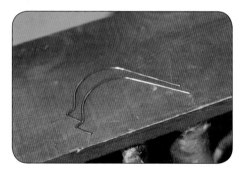

Step 1: Tools and Materials

The materials you will need will depend on how big and long you want your rack (or how much wood you have). I had enough wood to make a small one (15" long × 13" tall).

- ½" or ¾" plywood or hardwood
- Branching branches (I used 6.)
- Nails and/or screws (1" or so will do)
- 2 hanging hooks

Step 2: Cut and Trim the Branches

Cut your branches to the appropriate height of your rack. I cut mine to be approximately 12". Trim the bottoms and tops of the branches if needed to make the branches stand upright. If you have a branch or two that has a weird lean or curve to it, leave it— it adds character. One of my branches

65

had two branching sections (double the usage!). Also, if desired, trim the ends of the branching sections where your coat will hang.

Step 3: Cut the Boards for the Frame

Using your miter, table, chop, or handsaw, cut the boards to make the frame. My frame was approximately 8" deep, 15" long, and 13" tall.

Step 4: Attach Branches to the Frame

Using nails or screws, attach the branches to the bottom of the frame first (or the top; the order doesn't matter). If you are using screws, it may be useful to pre-drill the holes first.

Step 5: Finish the Frame and Secure Branches

After you have attached your branches to the bottom of the frame, attach the sides of the frame using screws or nails. Then attach the top of the frame. Secure the top of the branches to the frame with nails or screws.

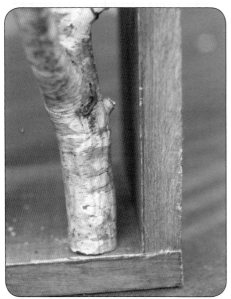

The wood I used was already quite old, so I didn't have to do anything.

Hang it up using the two hanging hooks (you know the "As Seen on TV" hooks). I found they are actually pretty useful and durable, especially when you don't have any studs.

Besides a rack, this also serves as a shelf! This is a small prototype. Later on, I may build a longer one.

Step 6: Finishing touches

Sand off any protruding edges. Use wood sealant or varnish to protect your new coat rack. If you want a "vintage" look to it, you could try putting some dents in the side with a hammer or nail.

decorate

Desktop 3D String Art

By peguiono
(http://www.instructables.com/
id/Desktop-3D-String-Art/)

Back in geometry class, we used to draw these on paper. I could never remember what they were actually called, but I think they went by "string art." (That's what came up in a search, too.)

Basically the idea is making a curve with straight lines. Usually it's done on paper or "stitched" onto cardboard. The plan for this one was to make a 3D version that I could hang on the wall or display on my desk. I think it turned out awesome, so I hope you like it.

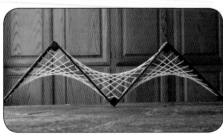

Step 1: Tools and Materials
Tools
- Drill
- ³⁄₁₆" drill bit
- Pencil (writing utensil)
- Tape measure or ruler

- Heavy duty stapler (This part is optional; you could just use glue alone, but you would need something else as an anchor then.)
- Saw (I used a coping saw, but any fine-toothed saw should work; you don't need to cut much.)
- Clamps will be a big help, especially if you're just using glue.

Materials
- About 4' of ¾" screen molding (also sold as plywood edging); this is the wood frame of the project.
- A roll of string (I used mason line.)
- Staples (if you're using them)
- A piece of scrap wood that's about ½" thick
- Paint (optional of course)

Step 2: Measure and Cut the Frame

This part is fairly easy; just take your tape measure or ruler and mark out four 9" sections of edging. Once you're done marking it, take your saw and cut out the four sections. See, that was simple enough.

Step 3: Mark It for Drilling

Start off by making marks every ¾". I made the first mark on the 1" and the last mark before 8", so there are ten marks in total. Go ahead and mark the same marks on the other three. For the edging, I'm using ¾" so the middle of it is ⅜". Make that mark on both sides and trace a line down the middle with a straightedge. Now you're ready to drill it.

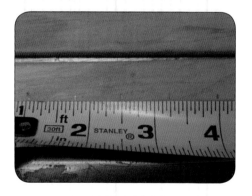

Step 5: Start Assembling

Now you're going to need that scrap piece of wood. Cut three pieces of the scrap that are about ¾" long (same width as the edging wood). Now put plenty of glue on the scrap pieces and create the 90° L shape (pictures help on this step). If you're stapling them, now is the time to do it; if not, then you should probably clamp them and let them dry before you do anything. You should have two L shapes now.

Step 4: Vroom Vroom, Drill It

This step speaks for itself pretty much. Stay on the middle line and drill a hole with the ³⁄₁₆" bit at each mark. It should give you a fairly consistent line of holes. It doesn't have to be perfect, but if you want to, you could use a drill press (I used a regular drill). You're drilling all the way through it, so drill on a scrap piece of wood.

decorate

Step 7: Strengthen It Up

(You should do this before you leave it to dry.) If you haven't noticed yet, it's pretty fragile. So what you can do is fill all the gaps with glue. The wood absorbs a lot of glue and it leaves gaps. Fill the gaps with glue. Then let it dry.

Step 6: Make the "W"

This part is probably the hardest part of the whole thing. Clamps and glue will be your best friends on this one. Put lots of glue on the third scrap piece and attach it to one of the Ls. If you're not stapling them, then you should clamp it here and let it dry completely before you attach the next one.

Now attach the other L to the scrap block with plenty of glue. This is the time to clamp everything up and let it dry for an hour or two. (If you didn't use staples, I would let it go overnight.) **Before leaving it to dry, read the next step.**

decorate

Step 8: Paint It (Optional)

Now that the glue is dry, if you are going to paint the frame, now's the time. I went with a glossy black; you can go with whatever color you want. I think neon colors would look pretty sweet.

Step 9: Time to String It

This is the time consuming step. You're going to need lots of string. There are two ways you can do this: You can string the whole thing in one consecutive piece or you can do ten separate strings. I did it in one consecutive string. So that's what I'm going to show you how to do. Start by pulling out a *lot* of string (25' or so). There would be nothing worse than stringing the whole thing and then being 5" short at the end. I used just shy of 25' of string—it's way better to have extra.

Pick one side and anchor one end of the string. I did this by tying a loop knot and stapling the knot (picture might help). Now you have to start threading everything. Start at the top hole, string it down to the closest hole at the bottom, and pull it all the way through (yes, this takes some time). Now take the end and thread it through the next hole out to the next highest hole, and pull it all the way through again. (This is somewhat confusing; the picture helps.)

Continue this pattern until you have the first L stitched up. After this, it gets a little trickier, but the next step explains it. **Stringing Tip:** If you hold the tip that you're threading with while you pull everything through, the line will never actually knot.

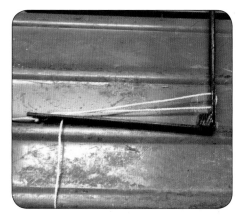

Step 10: Just Keep Stringing...

Once you finish the first one, it gets a little tricky. You're going to start sharing the holes. Same threading idea, it just takes a little bit more work. When you're done with the first L, the next step is to get the string to the next L thread in through the top hole of the following L (see picture). Then just keep going with the same pattern. The pictures really do a better job of explaining; it's kind of complicated. Look at them.

Once you finish the second L, the third L is just like the second. Go from the end of the second L and thread to the hole at the start of the third L. This is the same thing as going from the first L to the second one.

Step 11: Finishing Up

Now all three Ls are done! You could just staple it and tie it off right next to the hole, but I wanted mine to look the same on both sides. (Well, sort of). So I pulled everything tight and wrapped it around to the top and I anchored it there.

Now, go display your work of art on your desk or wall!

decorate

Section 3

Backyard

Want a DIY way to cook food *without* using fossil fuel LP or having to buy charcoal? I know I did. That's why I built a rocket grill! This is just one variation of a "rocket stove"—a simple appropriate technology for cleanly burning bio-fuels.

The rocket grill is fired by twigs, wood scraps, wood chips, or nearly anything else you can put in it. It naturally drafts air to maximize combustion. Once the grill is really going, no smoke comes out the top, only heat, and the grill really does sound like a rocket!

The grill is designed to not only grill, but also boil, bake, braise, and roast! Because of the simple design and robust construction, it is nearly maintenance free. Unlike an LP grill, the burner will never burn and rust away to nothingness (and cost good time and money to replace). There is no piezo-electric starter or other "modern" technology in the grill, which would be prone to failure.

Despite how it looks, the grill is small and light enough for one grown man to lift into the back of a pickup truck. That way, you can travel with it for camping or tailgating. (The lid and side tables are also removable for storage and easy packing.) Because it's covered and enclosed, it also qualifies for use as a "backyard fire-pit" in areas that do not allow open fires.

This project is mostly simple metal work. While it does require welding, it's pretty straight forward. This was really my first-ever welding project. So let's gather together our tools and materials and get started!

backyard

Step 1: Tools and Materials

Tools
- Angle grinder
- Grinding disc
- Cut-off disc
- Welder
- Safety glasses, work gloves, welding gloves, welding helmet, hearing protection
- Drill and drill bits
- Laser level, bubble level (optional)

Materials

This project is made mostly from scrap metal but will need several other parts.

Parts for the Grill Itself
- A base or something for the grill to stand on. Must be heatproof. I used a scrap steel farm implement disc.

- Steel pipe—diameter of your choice, but it will affect cooking size and fuel rate. I used 6.5" diameter scrap steel pipe, about 3' in length.
- Steel water tank (This becomes the "bowl" top of the grill and cooking surface area.)
- 4 pieces of small diameter steel pipe, about 6" in length
- 2 90° pipe elbows of same diameter
- 2 pipe flanges of same diameter
- 2 pieces of flat material that you like to make side countertop surfaces
- Small scraps of steel plate

Parts for the Lid of the Grill

- A piece of wood, species of your choice, sized for a lid handle
- 2 carriage bolts (about 5" long) with matching nuts and washers. Stainless steel is ideal, as these will be exposed to both heat and the elements. Plain steel is fine as a lower cost alternative.
- 2 pieces of copper or steel tube or pipe, slightly larger diameter and shorter length than the carriage bolts, to use as spacers
- The top end of the water tank

Other Items

- Steel plate, about 6" side × 12" long (perforations or slotted is ideal)
- JB Weld epoxy

First, gather together your materials for the main section of the rocket grill.

- Base
- Large diameter pipe
- Water tank

The base needs to be large enough to keep the whole grill from tipping over. It also forms the very end bottom of the grill, which hot coals and ashes will fall into. Any sort of steel plate would work fine. I found a piece of old farm machinery that fit the bill. It's a domed disc about 16" in diameter.

The large diameter pipe needs to be cut into two sections. Make one about 1', and the other about 20" long. The 20" section will be the "vertical tube," and the 1' section will be the "feeder tube."

That water tank that I chose was 16" in diameter. It was already cut apart from a solar water experiment I worked on. The bottom section of the tank is cut to about 1' tall. This becomes the cooking area "bowl" top to the grill. The water tank was also chosen because it is large enough in diameter to fit my camping cast iron Dutch oven and a stock pot that I use for boiling corn.

Stacked up, the base, vertical tube, and water tank section should come to a comfortable standing height for you. The top of the water tank section is the height that grilling will take place.

To cut the steel, I found that an angle-grinder with a cut-off disc works best. I made cuts quickly, without removing to much metal, and made a nice, straight line. You could also use a reciprocating saw with a metal cutting blade or a plasma-cutter if you have access to one.

To mark a line on a cylindrical object like the pipe or water tank, wrap a straight section of sheet metal around it, and secure with masking or duct tape. Mark this line with a permanent marking pen, then remove the sheet metal.

Cut the pipes and water tank to length, using common-sense safety precautions. (Wear work gloves, eye and hearing protection, etc.) Cut the top off the water tank and save to make the lid.

Stack up the base, vertical pipe, and water tank section to get a feel for how your grill will look. If you were working on a level surface, like a concrete garage floor, you can use a bubble level to make sure your vertical pipe is perfectly straight up and down. (Plumb!)

backyard

of an angle will not allow for proper air-flow and can prevent the grill from drafting properly.

Cutting the two pipes to fit together can be geometrically-challenging. An angle-grinder makes straight cuts, but both pipes are rounded. Still, they have to meet together tight enough to get a good weld between them. What you need to do is imagine how two straight cuts would look projected onto two curved surfaces. One easy way to do this is to use a laser level that has the ability to project a straight line. Several inches up from the end, point the laser at the vertical pipe, at the angle you want the feeder pipe to meet it. Then mark the laser line with your permanent marker. Rotate the laser 90° and mark the line again.

On the feeder pipe, mark two lines at 90° from each other the same way. Another way to mark the same cuts is to use sheet metal, which you can wrap around the pipes. It is possible to make a projection of what the cuts should look like, and cut that out of the sheet metal. Then wrap the sheet metal around the pipe and mark it. A friend of mine already had made a sheet metal template, so that's the technique I used.

When you are done, you will have a notch in the vertical pipe and a "bird's beak" cut in the feeder pipe. Fit the two pipes together, and see how close they match up. It's more that likely that you will need to use a grinder to get the parts to fit together well.

Step 2: The Special Cut

The most distinct feature of the Rocket Grill is how the feeder pipe and vertical pipe come together. While the exact angle that they connect at isn't super important, it should be somewhere between 90° and 45°. Having this connection at some angle makes it easier to feed fuel and prevents it from bending over too far. Too steep

backyard

Step 3: Welding

Weld together the vertical and feeder pipes. That's easiest to do with both pipes lying flat and sideways. Weld around one side, then flip it over, and weld the other side.

Next, stand the Y of pipes on top of the base. Make sure it is centered and that it is plumb and level. Weld the pipes to the base. (Make sure to always brush down the metal where you will be welding, and where the ground clamp connects.)

The bottom of the water tank needs a hole cut in it, the same diameter as

backyard

the vertical pipe. Mark that diameter hole on the bottom. One way to do that is just set the other parts right on top of the tank and trace it. Then cut the hole in the bottom of the tank. I had a plasma-cutter at a friend's house, so I used that. Otherwise, a cut-off disc, Sawzall, or large diameter hole-saw could work.

Stack the whole grill together upside down and weld the vertical tube to the water tank section. Again, make sure the parts are plumb and level. If there is a "front" to the water tank, make sure it's where you want it to be. On mine, there were two pipe ports that I wanted to be left and right, with the feeder tube on an angle to my right as I faced it.

At this point, the basic grill is done, but we still need the lid and a few other details.

backyard

backyard

Step 4: Fuel/Air Plate

Another distinct feature of the Rocket Grill is the fuel/air plate. It holds the fuel up and in place, and it allows plenty of air to naturally draft into the grill and up through the fuel for a very hot and clean burn. The plate needs to be able to hold up to high temperatures.

Take some scrap steel plate and cut it to a width just slightly smaller than the diameter of the feeder pipe and about the same length. This way, the plate sits *inside* the feeder pipe and divides it to an upper and lower area. Fuel goes in *above* the plate and air goes in *below* the plate. The plate has holes or slots in it in the far end so that it supports the fuel but allows plenty of air through. The plate I used was already slotted, but I added a few more for good measure. You could also use a heavy-duty grate, or weld together re-bar to serve the same purpose. When you are ready, just slide the plate into the feeder tube. Gravity and friction will hold it in place for you.

Step 5: Building the Lid

When I cut the water tank apart, I also cut off the top and saved it for use as a lid. It's already the same diameter as the top of the grill, so it should fit perfect. It really just needs two modifications: a handle and a way to let air through.

The Handle

The length and width of the handle is based on the size of the user's hand, preferably with enough room for an oven mitt. I found a scrap of oak firewood, about the right diameter for a handle, and left it long to start with. I could always shorten it later. Drill two holes in the wood, and push the carriage bolts through. Use these to mark where they should go through on the lid. Drill two holes in the lid.

Cut two sections of pipe a little shorter than the length of the carriage bolts. These will be spacers to hold the handle the right distance from the lid. I had some scrap copper pipe around, which is easy to cut and looks very nice. Slide a washer and then the pipe over the carriage bolts, and then place the carriage bolts into the holes in the lid. On the bottom side of the lid, attach washers and nuts and tighten.

Air Spacers

The lid also needs some way for hot air to constantly exit the grill to continue the chimney effect. You could make a vent, similar to one like a Weber brand grill or even some sort of chimney right on the lid, but it seemed much easier just to add some small steel tabs. These tabs space the lid away from the grill to allow air flow. I cut three steel tabs from scrap metal and welded them evenly around the lid.

On the inside of the grill, I welded in three matching tabs that line up with the ones on the lid. Three tabs keep the lid from wobbling. By simply rotating the lid a little, it can still sit all the way down on the grill (such as when you are done with the grill and want to smother it or for storage).

backyard

Step 6: Side Tables

What's a grill without some workspace to hold your utensils, your plate of meat, and your favorite beer? That's why the grill needs side tables.

The water pressure tank used to make the top of the grill included pipe connections in the sides. I purchased just a couple short sections of pipe and elbows so that these could support the side tables. I threaded in a horizontal pipe into each side, and then I inserted a 90° elbow into that. A vertical pipe section then completes an L on either side of the grill.

Both side tables have a pipe flange going to a short piece of pipe smaller in diameter than the vertical side pipe. That way, the side table pipe sits inside the vertical pipe. This makes it easy to remove the side tables for travel. Drilling a hole through both pipes allows me to slide a small bolt through, preventing the side table from accidentally rotating.

At first, I wasn't sure what I wanted to use for the top surface of the side tables. I dug through my pile of scrap/salvaged/recycled materials and found an assortment of stone, tile, steel, aluminum, and wood. I simply set different pieces of materials on top of the side-arm pipes to see what looked good. In the end, I decided on a blue/green slate stone for the left side, and a steel deck place for the right side.

For the steel on the right, I just welded the pipe flange to the bottom of it, threaded in the short section of pipe, and slid that into the slightly larger diameter vertical pipe. A horizontally-drilled hole with a bolt slid through it completed that side.

The slate for the left was a little more work. The slate was rough and pointed, but it is a very soft stone. I experimented and found that rubbing the edges of the stone with a cold chisel allowed me to shape the stone a bit and smooth the rough edges.

To attach the stone to the side pipe, I found some scrap metal about the right size for the bottom of the stone side table. I welded the pipe flange to the bottom of the metal and then glued that to stone with a tube of JB WELD adhesive. Again, the pipe on the side table just slides into the vertical pipe on the side of the grill.

Step 7: Odds and Ends

Paint Removal

The water tank section of the grill is painted, and the paint had to be removed before using the grill for cooking. I thought about what the most "eco-friendly" way to remove all the paint was. I thought about all the nasty chemicals used as paint strippers. In the end, I decided make a very hot test fire to both try out the grill and remove the paint. The paint easily peeled off.

Pot Bracket

To hold either the stock pot or Dutch oven, there still needs to be air space in the bottom of the grill. The easiest answer was just to span the fire tube with two short sections of slotted C-channel. They support the pot and let plenty of heat and air through. They are not welded in place. I didn't see any reason to, and this way they are removable.

Heat Diffuser

One downside of this grill design is that it gets an extreme hot-spot in the middle of the grill and is much cooler towards the outside edge. That's a bad thing for cooking burgers and sausages. So I put in a "heat diffuser" when grilling. It's just a small steel plate that I practiced welding on before welding the grill together. It simply sits directly on the pot bracket and works well to spread out the heat. At some point, I may make a more aesthetically-pleasing heat spreader, but this one works fine for now.

Ash Cleanout

You may have noticed that there is no ash cleanout on the grill. In truth, I really haven't seen a design for one that I like. I have seen similar steel rocket stoves that use a threaded pipe port, which seems like it would gunk up the threads easy. Also a large diameter pipe port gets expensive quickly, and I was trying to use as many free, inexpensive, and recycled parts as possible. For now, I just flip the whole grill upside down to empty the ash. It makes far less ash than you might think. In the future, I may use the angle grinder to cut an angle out of the bottom back side of the grill and then hinge it, so that there is a flip-up flap to access and empty the ash.

Grill Grate

The grate is just a standard round grill grate. It's the medium size. It actually overlaps the top of the grill, which makes it easier to use the entire top. Downside? It's easier to slide a burger right off the top of the grill as well!

Step 8: Fueling and Firing

One of the best things about the Rocket Grill is how it's fueled. No longer do I have to purchase fossil-fuels to cook my backyard fare! Because of the amount of air that flows through the grill, almost any bio-fuel burns great in it. This one is really designed for twigs and sticks.

After every wind storm, all of my neighbor's trees shed their sticks downwind into my yard. Before, I would grumble at the yard-work of picking up all those sticks and moving them back to the brush pile. Now, I instead gather them up looking forward to burgers,

corn on the cob, or whatever I am going to cook up next.

To start the grill, I just put a little bit of tinder (usually a bit of newspaper) and a few twigs onto the far end of the fuel/air plate. I light it with a match or cigarette lighter and then just feed in a few more twigs. After that, a fair amount of sticks, firewood, or other fuel can be loaded on the top side of the fuel plate.

The fire is very simple to light and starts right up. Even *extra long* fuel can go right in. Just slide it a little farther in every once in a while. The chimney effect makes all the heat go up the vertical tube. No smoke or fire comes out the feeder tube.

I am right-handed, so I designed the grill so that the feeder tube comes out on an angle to the right. That way, it is easy for me to fuel, but I don't hit my shin on it. Since pots sit down inside the grill when boiling, the heat transfer of the fire to the pot is very good. The heat hits not just the bottom of the pot but travels up the sides as well. This means you get a boil going faster, while using less fuel.

I also used my grill in a rain storm a while back. My concern was rain running down the lid and then inside the grill. It wasn't an issue any rain hitting the lid simply vaporized or sizzled right off!

Step 9: Grill It Up!

So far, I have used the grill for chicken, burgers, brats and sausages, corn on the cob, shish kebab, and more. The design also allows me to boil in the stock pot or bake in the Dutch oven. (I'm working on baked desserts now, too!)

A friend of mine has designed both a giant skillet and a very nice wok for his. Another possible future modification is to create a high-thermal mass pizza oven top for the grill.

Rocket stoves lend themselves well to infinite variation and re-use of existing materials. Combine that with versatility and efficient use of fuel, and you have the cook stove of tomorrow, today.

Remember, this isn't rocket science, just good use of appropriate technology! I hope you find my Rocket Grill to be inspirational. You too can cook net-carbon-zero deliciousness over open flames and take pride in your own design.

Sand Fire Garden

By jonsarriugarte
(http://www.instructables.com/
id/Sand-Fire-Garden/)

backyard

So many people who have hung out with the warmth and played in the sand of my wonderful Fire Gardens have asked me how they could make one of their own. This Instructable will walk you though the basics of building your very own Zen Fire Garden. You will need to find or make your own container and build a stand or a base.

Step 1: Plumbing Parts

You will needs some basic off-the-shelf parts to make a fire pit;

* Regulator/hose 30 PSI (not a BBQ regulator) and a needle valve to adjust the flame size (I use brass ⅜" 45° flair fitting for the hose ends and the attachment at the fire pit.)
* Fire ring—this is the distribution system that is below the sand for your gas. If you have the ability to weld and make rings, you can make your own using a ½" weldable (not cast iron) coupler in the center and ⅝" thin wall tubing and drilling ³⁄₃₂ " holes every 1.5". The ring should be half the size to one third

the size of your container diameter.

Stainless steel will prolong the life of the ring, especially during the winter when you forget to cover your pit in the first rain.

* Fittings—½" NPT coupler (weldable), brass ½" to ⅜" 45° flare (for attaching the hose to, not used in this build), brass ½" NPT nipple (to attach the ring to the coupler welded to the container, also not used in this build), brass ½" NPT lock nut
* BBQ-sized propane tank

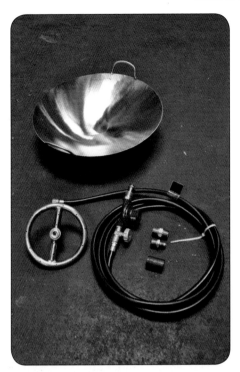

Step 2: Container for the Fire Pit

With a little searching through your local hardware store, garden center, junkyard, or restaurant supply you can find great ready-made vessels to build your own custom fire garden in.

In addition to the plumbing parts, you will need a container that is able to handle high temperatures and be fully sealed underneath (leaks or drain holes will also allow gas out and fire where you don't want it). The bottom 6"–8" of a 55-gallon drum works good. I have also used a wok, stainless salad bowl, or dog bowls. Stay away from painted steel, aluminum, and galvanized steel, as these will release fumes or melt. The weldable coupler can be welded though the bottom. I have seen people make these in cement, ceramic pots, and I have used mine with a 3' pipe added right in the beach sand (to move the hose away from the heat).

Step 3: Adding a Hole for the Plumbing

Locate and mark the center of the wok, then center punch. Make sure you are center punching with a hard object backing up the other side. If you aren't, your mark will be too light and you risk just making a big dent. Now, using a step drill like in picture 2, drill a ⅞" hole. If you find the bit wandering off center, go back and make a better center punch. Stainless steel is very hard and lots of pressure is needed to get the first hole on the step drill. Step drills are a great way to make round holes in thin materials. Normal drills tend to make oblong holes in thin materials and a large hole is really not recommended with standard drill bits. A step drill can be found at your local hardware store in the drill section or in the electrical area for making knock outs for EMT conduit. They are not cheap; a more economical solution is a hole saw. These come in the different sizes. Use ⅞" for the set nut or 1⅛" hole for the bolt-in and weld-in coupler.

Step 4: Adding the Plumbing

For this build, I use a brass ½" NPT × ⅜" 45° flare fitting with a brass ½" NPT set nut. It fit snug in the hole and needed no additional sealant or welding. I used gas Teflon tape on the brass, slipped it through the hole, and threaded the ring to it on the inside. Use a wrench to make sure it's tight. Make sure the holes are pointed down so the sand doesn't run in.

Alternates methods of plumbing the gas though the container for thicker materials:

- Bolt on flange—great for thick material. Make sure to use a high-temperature silicon sealer to make sure there are no leaks.
- Weldable coupler—the best solution, but you must be able to weld.

Now attach the hose/regulator using the 45° flare fitting on the end of your hose.

Step 5: Making a Stand

I used a ½" × ¼" steel strap for both the ring and legs. I first rolled the steel in a slip roll. This could also be done with a bending fork. You can make one with a vise by clamping two bolts ⅜" apart. Now leverage the steel between and bump (small bend, move, ½" bend again) till you have a ring. Weld the ends together, then true it up with a hammer.

I then cut three 16" pieces and hammered the end flat on the anvil. Using the bending fork, I bent the legs to match my drawing. Now divide the ring into three and tack weld each leg to it. Now you can true up each leg to be square to the ring and to land the same distance from the center of the ring. Now weld solid. I finish mine with paint. If you can't weld, get creative with plumbing parts, bolt on legs, set it into a metal bucket, and inputting a cement pit are just a few ideas.

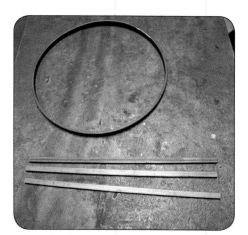

Step 6: Add the Sand

Set on top of your new stand, hook up the regulator to the propane BBQ tank, and add sand. Sand should be 3" to 4" above the ring. I use playground washed sand from the hardware store.

This is a match light system and I like plumbing torches or BBQ lighters to light mine. Light the torch, then turn on the gas with the flame above the sand. It will take several seconds for the sand to fill with gas and rise to the top. Now, use the needle valve to adjust the flame. Once lit it's time to play in the sand with simple tools. This works best after dark when you can turn the flame down very low until you only see a blue flame.

Notes

- Do not ever touch the sand with your hands or any other part of your body! It will stick and burn you. Use caution, common sense, and remember that fire is hot!
- Don't worry about fire traveling up the hose, but do make sure your fittings are leak proof (soapy water is a good way to test).
- Keep your tank as far away as possible from your pit.

backyard

Propane/NG Disclaimer
Book Disclaimer

This Instructable is for informational purposes only. It is not intended to be an instructional medium of any type. Nor is it intended to be an authority regarding safety or regulatory issues. It is not intended to be a guide for safety or security. This Instructable is designed to introduce current and prospective users of propane to common issues in the use of propane and as an explanation of how propane tanks, LP/NG Gas parts, and related appurtenances operate and what their purpose is. Using this book as a guide for diagnosing problems or attempting to fix propane related problems is, under no circumstance whatsoever, advised or recommended. Only licensed propane companies and/ or LP Gas plumbers are to diagnose and make repairs. This site assumes no liability as it is intended for educational and informational purposes only.

I do not endorse any particular safety procedure or policy but rather endorse the practice of overall safety and common sense regarding all aspects of propane/NG and its properties. This book is not intended for "do it yourself" consumers or as a guide for unlicensed propane plumbing activity. It is published solely as a resource for people seeking information about propane and to better understand the activities that licensed propane companies, installers, and plumbers are engaged in.

Photography and Content Disclaimer

Be aware that safety rules and regulations vary among states and jurisdictions. Although the nationally recognized standards of NFPA 58 and NFPA 54 govern the propane industry on a national level, independent states, counties, cities, and locales often have their own rules and regulations concerning LP/NG Gas and propane. The content within the Instructables' site,

along with the pictures, depict an overall view of safety as an exhibit. The content and pictures within this Instructable are not intended as a guide, but rather as an exhibit. Rules and regulations reside with individual states and local jurisdictions, not with the contextual or photographic depictions within the Instructables' site.

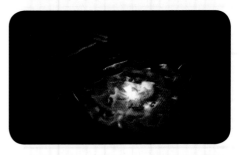

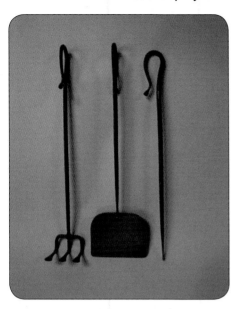

Step 7: Examples of my Fire Gardens

These fire gardens all use the same basic plumbing system. Visit www.fireishot.com to view more.

Concrete Cylinders from Cardboard Tubes

By CHENG Concrete
(http://www.instructables.com/
id/Concrete-Cylinders-from-
Cardboard-Tubes/)

Tools
- Permanent marker
- Tin snips/wire cutters
- Long needle-nose pliers
- Phillips screwdriver (+)
- Scissors
- Weights/rocks/sand
- Diamond sanding pad/sandpaper

Safety
- Particle mask
- Rubber gloves

This Instructable will explain how to make concrete cylinders using discarded cardboard packaging tubes (potato chips, ground coffee, mixed nuts, baby formula, etc.).

Difficulty Level: Beginner.

Materials
- 2 cardboard tubes (best with foil or plastic linings for water resistance)
- 4 1" screws
- Clear packing tape
- Thin foam wrap (a packing/shipping material)
- Sacked concrete/rapid set (if you're in a hurry, although it tends to wash out colors)
- CHENG Pro-Formula Mix

Step 1: Prepare Tubes

These tubes were found in recycling bins at a nearby apartment complex. It might take a few trips to find the right sizes, but keep looking because they're being thrown away all the time.

The largest tube will become the outside form. In this case, it's about 5" diameter and 9" tall (it contained coffee grounds). The inside tube is about 4" × 7" (shredded potato chip container). This means the wall thickness is only about ½"—do not go any thinner, this is already pushing the limits.

Starting with the interior form, trace the diameter on a piece of thin foam

padding (this is usually used for packing/shipping). The idea is to tape a circle of foam to the base so, when we go to de-mold, that metal ring isn't trapped down inside. After the foam circle is taped to the base, cut about a 2" foam strip to wrap and tape around the bottom edge (to keep that ring from getting trapped).

Screw the four 1" screws into the top of the interior form. The screws should rest on the lip of the outer cylinder, helping to keep it lined up during the pour. Clean up the forms, inside and ut, and remove any oils or residue with denatured alcohol. If you don't clean the containers out, you'll see it on the surface of the finished concrete for sure.

Step 2: Mix, Pour, and Vibrate Concrete

In a clean bucket, mix up some concrete. If you're using CHENG Pro-Formula, follow the directions on the box. Pro-Formula comes in a range of colors, is easy to use, and gives good results. The mix in these photos looks a bit too wet. A mix that's too wet won't be as strong, but for a small project like this it won't make much difference. Fill the outer cylinder with concrete first, smearing concrete around the inside surface as you go along. This will help the concrete fill the edges and should minimize air bubbles.

With the outer cylinder about half full, wipe the exterior of the inside cylinder with concrete and gradually push it down into the form. The concrete will be displaced and spill up out of the edges. Take some weights (lead, solid metal, stones, sand, etc.) and put them into the interior form. You want to offset the buoyant force of the fluid concrete. Too much weight and the inside form will sink (and bend the locating screws). Not enough weight and the inside cylinder will want to float up.

backyard

Vibrate the form by lifting it and dropping it repeatedly on the work surface (this is called drop compaction). Do this for a few minutes to help coax the air bubbles into rising to the surface. With your vibrating finished, make sure the inner cylinder is centered within the outer one. Then move it gently to a quit place where it will be undisturbed. Cover the piece with plastic and let it cure for one to two days.

Step 3: De-Mold

Scrape away concrete from the top edge and snip the metal ring, gradually peeling the cardboard away. Hopefully the metal ring from the inner cylinder isn't trapped. Use some long needle-nose pliers if it is, although sometimes things just get stuck. There's not much to this; just be careful not to cut yourself on the metal rings, and remember not to pry against the concrete because you'll just scratch it.

Step 4: Grind, Polish, Seal

Take a diamond hand pad or sandpaper and clean up any sharp edges. The top surface will be a bit rough, and if you don't have a 5" orbital polisher, you might try sanding it with 60-grit sandpaper on a rubber pad or fixed to

a block of wood. It will take forever, but you can get it looking decent if you're patient. You can also grind and polish concrete using the same equipment you would use to grind and polish glass. At this step, you'll get the best results if you have the right tool for the job (5" orbital polisher with pads for concrete).

These next steps are optional. Seal the concrete with something like the CHENG Acrylic Sealer. Sealing concrete is a whole other thing, but there's some step by step information at concreteexchange.com. Sealing isn't necessary, but it will protect the concrete and keep it looking good over the long term. If the cylinder is going to be a planter, drill a ½" hole in the bottom with a masonry bit.

Step 5: Variations

Here is the same process using smaller cardboard tubes. In this case the potato chip tube was cut down to fit. Sand was used as the ballast to keep the inside tube from floating in the wet concrete. This piece hasn't been ground, and the top surface is how it came out of the form. If the outside tube has a metal lip, the concrete will fill to that edge and the top surface will be nice and flat.

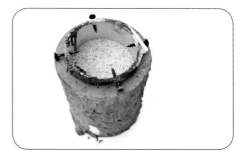

backyard

on any metal. In retrospect, wiping off the concrete while it's wet would have made this de-molding process a lot less messy. Completely remove the form tubes and then pry out the cork knockout with a small slotted screwdriver. Try not to use the edge of the hole for leverage—it will damage the concrete. Instead, drive the screw driver into the cork and force it up without prying on the concrete.

In this piece, the knockout didn't make complete contact with the bottom of the tube, and ⅛" of concrete was filling the hole. This was simply tapped away with a rubber mallet and a slotted screwdriver. The edges can be sanded with diamond hand pads and then the piece is ready to be finished or potted with a plant as is.

Step 6: More Advanced: Use a Wine Cork to Cast a Drain Hole

To make the drain hole for a small concrete planter like these cylinders, we could always drill the hole with a masonry bit, but it's cleaner to cast the hole instead. It's easy, less dusty, and you can just use a wine cork.

Determine how thick the bottom of the piece will be, and then cut the cork to that thickness. In this case it's a little bit over ½". Mark the cut line around the cork and use a utility knife or a fine-toothed handsaw to cut it. Mark the center of the tube, spray both faces of the cork, and press it in place, making sure it stays centered. Let the adhesive dry before starting the pour. The interior tube should now rest on top of the cork (it needs to make complete contact with the bottom of the tube to create the hole).

Mix, pour, and vibrate the concrete. To eliminate the most air bubbles, use a small vibrating table or a table-mounted vibrator. Remove lead weights and de-mold the finished concrete using tin snips and pliers. Be careful not to cut yourself

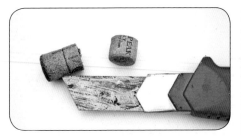

Step 7: Final Photos

These concrete cylinders are fun to make, and it's an easy way to start playing with concrete. Large concrete form tubes are used for construction, and the cardboard cylinders you find in the trash are basically scaled-way-down versions. Although they might not make very good containers for food, with a cork lid or a wooden top you've got a nice little vessel for holding whatever.

concrete cylinders from cardboard tubes

Building birdhouses is one of those classic things to do with your hands. We are first exposed to the process in high school wood class. Frustrating moments with poorly fitting plywood and nails usually end any interest in the project. This is a new twist on the design for these usually dull construction projects that will actually look good on the outside of your house this summer and involves fun construction techniques uncommon for this type of project. The process uses bendable poplar wood plywood that is made in Italy and is available at most specialty wood shops, assembled in a composite epoxy-coated structure that is light, waterproof, and elegant.

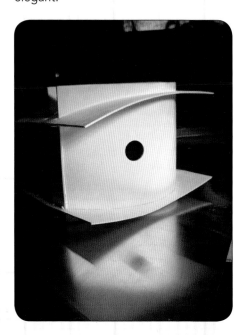

Step 1: Tools and Materials
- Bendable poplar plywood 4" × 8" sheet—about $35
- West System 105-B Epoxy Resin 32 ounces
- West System 206-B Slow Hardener 27 ounces
- Foam brushes
- Craftsman or RotoZip cutter tool with ⅛" rotary blade for wood
- Razor blade knife with utility blade
- Shirt cardboard, four pieces 8" × 12"
- Elmer's carpenter's wood filler—interior/exterior
- Hot glue gun
- Sandpaper or sanding block
- Bits: ¼" and 1.5"
- Clamps

Step 2: Modeling the Birdhouse

This birdhouse design is a simple arrangement of four pieces of 8" × 12" bendable poplar plywood. I began with a model of the construction made up of four pieces of shirt cardboard—a construction material that I remember fondly from my childhood. These are still available from your shirts if you have them boxed and laundered; otherwise you can cut them out of "store bought" cardboard. The roof and the floor consist of identical cut designs that hold the curved sides in place. The curved cuts in the cardboard model should be centered mirror images of each other and should not extend further than ½" from the edges of the cardboard. The type of curve you draw and model are up to you, but the curve must be long enough to accommodate the length of the side pieces. In the model, you can cut the slits with a razor-knife; in the poplar you will be cutting the slits with a ⅛" RotoZip bit that will allow the plywood to slip in.

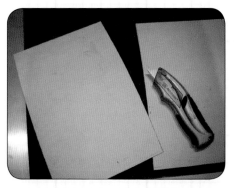

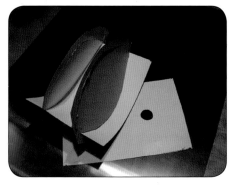

Step 3: Cutting the Pieces

There is a natural curve to the panel of plywood, and the four identical pieces of poplar plywood required in each birdhouse all should curve in their long dimension. The 8" × 12" pieces can be easily marked out on the large sheet so that you should get six pieces out of the 48" side of the sheet. The plywood is easily cut with a straightedge and a razor knife.

Step 4: Drawing the Cuts

The inspiration for the design of the birdhouse came from a wing shape that I had in my mind. I used a curve tool to get the shape I wanted and cut a piece of wood to use in tracing the line on the poplar plywood pieces. The lines were drawn so that they stopped ½" from the ends of the plywood and were mirrored across the long axis of the piece, staying 1" away at the ends. Other similar cuts can work and you can experiment with the design. Both the roof and the floor piece are drawn out in the exact same way.

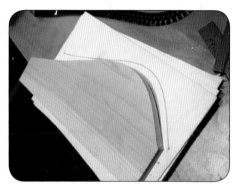

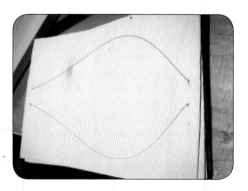

Step 5: Cutting the Groove

I usually cut both marked top and bottom at one time—if building multiple houses you can cut four of these sheets at one time. It is best to clamp the sheets securely before cutting. I drill start and stop holes at the end of each line with a ¼" bit and then proceed to cut out the long channels with the RotoZip or Craftsman equivalent rotary drill with the ⅛" bit. This will form the tight slot that will hold the wall pieces in place. It takes a little practice to get a smooth cut, but, if you are moving slowly, the line will be quite steady. This is an amazing piece of technology and useful for a lot of other projects.

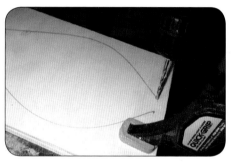

backyard

Step 6: Cut the Bird Hole

I used a 1.5" bit to cut this—the literature varies on this dimension and I won't get into it. The hole should be cut about halfway up the side in the portion which curves the least—you don't want to press your luck when you are bending this stuff; holes definitely weaken it. Only one of the side pieces gets a hole!

Step 7: Assembly

This is the fun part. This takes a little goofing with, but with a bit of gentle bending, you can get all the pieces together. Get the top or bottom on first and then move it down on the pieces to stabilize it before putting on the opposite one. After getting it roughly together, carefully adjust the top and bottom to match the wing-shaped curves of the sides.

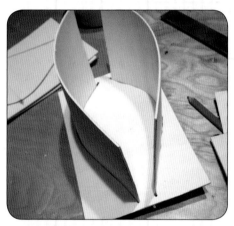

Step 8: Sealing It Up

Measure the openings on the two ends and cut side pieces to fit in these spaces out of the poplar plywood. The structure can be temporarily tacked together with a few dots of hot glue. The side and the top are self-tensioning

backyard

and usually don't require this—only the end pieces do.

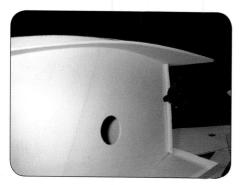

the two components and to apply it to the structure. Not only does it glue the whole thing together into a composite structure, it also forms a weather barrier to keep it going for many summers to come. Make sure you treat the end cuts of all the plywood. The stuff hardens overnight, and you'll have at least twenty minutes to put it on. Make sure you get the stuff into the cracks to glue and seal them. Only one coat of epoxy is necessary to seal and glue the structure. Wear latex gloves for this step.

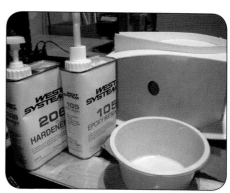

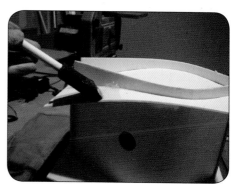

Step 9: Epoxy Coating

The West System is very nice. It usually includes the self measuring pumps attached to the hardener and the epoxy. If you haven't used epoxy systems before, you should read up on safety rules that come with the stuff. It is really easy to use and it takes about six pumps of each one to make a large enough batch to coat the whole structure. You use a sponge brush to mix

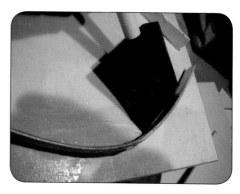

Step 10: Sealing and Sanding

There will be some openings in the structure once the epoxy dries. Seal these with some wood filler of the appropriate color. The structure can then be sanded to smooth out the small defects that occur when applying epoxy for the first or fortieth time. The final structure can then be left a natural color by applying a polyurethane finish or an appropriate outdoor paint.

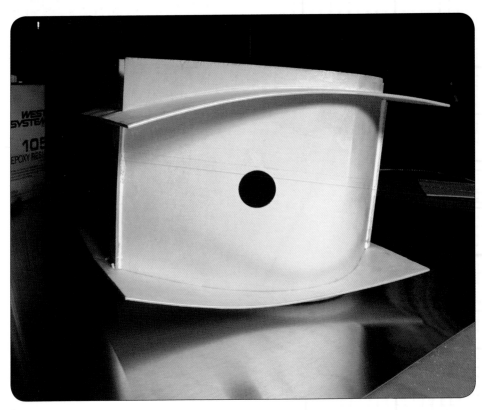

Step 11: Ready for the Birds

You may want to modify the design so you are able to remove one of the small end panels for cleaning between residents. You can also cut the square edges off with your rotary cutter tool. These structures are very fun to make, and modeling them with cardboard can get you a neat lunchbox or a variety of other bendable composite creations.

Disappearing Water Fountain

By DenVogel
(http://www.instructables.com/
id/Disappearing-Water-Fountain/)

This project is for building your own outdoor disappearing fountain (err . . . "water feature" as I guess they call it in the biz). We're not talking about a little pot with a trickle of water into a saucer. I'm not a fan of fountains that sound like someone peeing into a cup. We're shooting for an effect similar to a geyser shooting out of the ground. The basin will hold around 15 gallons and produce a noticeable gushing and splashing sound.

A disappearing fountain gives you the spray and sound of water, without the open pond. It can be a pretty cool visual effect, as the water will disappear into your base. The smaller water basin makes for a greener solution, requiring less water. This can be a good choice if you have children or pets that you don't want to worry about falling into a pond, and if you don't care about having plants or fish.

There are great-looking, ready-made fountains and fountain kits available on the market. Unfortunately, even a modest outdoor ready-made water feature starts at several hundred dollars and can easily run into the thousands. The pre-made components (e.g. basin) required to piece together your own creation really aren't any cheaper by the time you're done. Our goal is to build an in-ground fountain with inexpensive, easy to find materials. Depending on your specific needs, you can probably get it done for less than $100 ($200 including decorative rock).

Step 1: Materials and Tools

Let's make sure we have all the necessary tools and materials. The fewer trips we make to the hardware store, the better. Less money on gas means more money for beer! Obviously some of these items are optional. You're using power tools, so you must be an adult. Thus can you decide for yourself if you'd rather where safety glasses now, or an eye patch later.

Materials

Depending on your design, and where your fountain will be located, the size and quantity of materials you need may vary. Ours is a pretty simple geyser shooting out of rocks design. It will be about 20' from our power source.

- Basin (15 gallon HP15 $22.99)
- Pump Laguna 529 Gallon Per Hour (GPH) pond fountain PT8160 ($55.99)
- Sprinkler drip-system tap (½" riser adapter with ¼" barb—$1.49)
- Valve box, circular, 10" ($10.97)
- 2 electrical PVC conduits 1.25" × 10' ($3.72)
- 3 PVC sweep connectors 1.25" ($1.74)
- 2 PVC slip cap 1.25" ($.87)

109

- PVC glue ($2.29)
- Landscape fabric
- Sheet plastic or lawn garden bags
- Noiyo cobble decorative rock (1,000 lbs in bags—$82)
- 4 Rebar ¼" × 4' ($3.27)
- 2 Rebar ¼" × 3' ($2.78)
- Hardware mesh
- Spray primer gray ($4.59)
- Spray paint flat black ($4.49)

Tools
- Shovel
- Hack saw
- Dremel rotary cutting tool
- Pipe tape
- Gloves
- Safety glasses
- Knee pads
- Marking chalk (flour works too)
- Pressure washer *
- Dog *

Step 2: Site Prep

Make sure that you've cleared the area and have all your tools and supplies handy. It's a good idea to test your pump now before you go any further. Also make sure that your pump power cord will make it to an electrical outlet. Bigger pumps have cords that are 20' to 30'. Since you're mixing water and electricity, it would be best if your outlet had a GFCI breaker (Ground Fault Circuit Interrupter).

Spray marking chalk is a big help for designating where everything will run. Flour is a decent alternative to marking chalk if you don't want to spend the money or have pets that you'd rather not expose to the chalk.

We had an existing concrete slap with a dirt filled hole. This made a great place to contain our rock garden. It does add the challenge of running hose and power cord under concrete.

Step 3: Digging

Break out that shovel and start digging (or excavating if you want to sound like a pro). If you have a dog, let him help. Rock containment needs a few inches. Notice that we've taken down the dirt evenly across the surface. Make a basin hole so that it can sit with its top edge level with the ground. Our basin is about 9.25" in height.

You need a power cable trench if you're running your cable across the lawn. We chose to run our power cable inside an electrical conduit. It is easy to cut with a hack saw. The conduit might seem like overkill, but I think worth the extra effort. If your fountain is not near an outlet, it will hide the power cable. For me, seeing cables and wires ruins the effect. It will protect your pump cord from getting cut. If you ever need to replace your pump, you can just tie a

---

* Optional, but highly recommended

line on the power cord and pull the one for your new pump back through. No digging.

Next, we built a water-supply run. We have an existing sprinkler system and I decided to tap off of it so that the basin has a chance to refill every morning when the sprinklers run. Not all that splashing water will make it back into the basin, and I don't want to be refilling with a garden hose.

We had an existing slab, which adds the challenge of running hose and power cord under concrete. A pressure washer is great for blasting a path through dirt and gravel. Try to keep your under concrete run as small as possible, so you don't weaken its support and cause a crack. Tree roots are another story.

Step 4: Hook It Up

Line your hole and surrounding ground with landscape fabric. This will help limit weeds, but still allow any spill, splash, or rain water to get back into the ground. Place your pump in the center of the basin. Run your power cord to your electrical outlet (through the conduit if you're using it). Run your refill tube if you're utilizing one. Give it a test run. Fill the basin and plug it all in to ensure everything works before we start filling things back in.

backyard

Step 5: Support Grid

Build a support grid for your rock using rebar and hardware cloth. The rock required to cover a 5' diameter area weighs over 1,000 pounds. Elevating the rock above our basin lets us keep more water available for the pump, prevents the rock from crushing things, and gives us some wiggle room for the pump.

Make sure the rebar extends well past the width of your basin hole. Run at least two rebar cross members perpendicular to the other pieces and secure them with wire. Secure hardware cloth to the rebar with wire. Cut a hole in the center of your hardware cloth. This is where the fountain will spray through. Make sure the hole is large enough to fit your hand and the pump through should you need to reposition or replace it.

We chose to paint the support grid black. This will help minimize any rust and also made the grid less visible under our rock. A good coat of primer before painting will help protect the metal, and also give the paint something better to stick to than galvanized metal. Place your grid over your basin, with the pump extender tube centered in the hardware mesh hole. Be careful not to pinch your power cable or refill tube. There will be a lot of weight on the grid and won't be easy to move later.

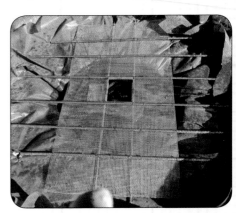

Step 6: Decorative Rock

We choose Noiyo cobble stones as ground over for our fountain. If you do not have a truck or wheel barrow, find a supplier that sells by the bag. It may cost a little more, but it will keep from tearing up your car and make it manageable to carry the rock to your fountain area.

Start placing stones in the center so that you can insure stable rock placement around the pump itself and adequate space for the fountain to spray up. Work your way out. We found it best to position flatter stones as a bottom layer, then use smaller round stones to fill in gaps. In the end, you do not notice any ground or support structure unless you look very hard.

Step 7: Site Cleanup

Fill in your trenches with dirt. If you dug under concrete, make sure that you pack your dirt and gravel material back under it as best as possible. It will help prevent cracking. If you have set aside your initial digging that has grass attached, put it back on top of your fill in dirt. Walk on it and give it a good watering. It will look rough for a while, but it will likely grow back in.

Step 8: Enjoy!

You now have a working disappearing water fountain!

Step 9: Other Costs
Electrical Costs

Consider the long-term cost of your pump. A cheap pump may require frequent replacement or use a lot of electricity, costing you more in the long run. You can estimate the electrical cost of running a pump by using this formula: amps × volts divided by 1000 × kWh cost × 24 hours-a-day × 30.4 days-per-month = cost per month. For example, a .45 Amp, 120 Volt pump at $0.17 per kWh that runs 24 hours 7 days a week will cost roughly $6.70 per month.

If the pump is rated in watts instead of amps, use this formula: watts divided by 1000 × kWh × 24 hours-a-day × 30.4 days-per-month. There are also some online pump-operating cost calculators that will help you.

backyard

Decorative Costs

Due to size of the area we needed to cover, and our choice of rock, the decoration ended up costing more than the fountain itself. You can certainly choose another type of ground cover, or even use a flower pot or some other type of vessel, to save some money and let your idea spring (pun intended) to life.

Step 10: Tips and Tricks

Here are some tips and tricks that might save you time and headaches.

- Use common sense. You're playing with tools, electricity, and water. Electricity and water can be a hazardous mix. Use cables and connectors designed for outdoor applications.
- Call before you dig. Particularly if you live in an urban or suburban area, there may be sewer, electrical, water, cable, phone lines, etc. buried on your property that you're not even aware of.
- Note that plants and fish have special water filter and treatment needs, which can add to the cost and complexity of your fountain.
- Pump should circulate half the volume of your pond every hour. So a 200-gallon pond requires at least a 100-gph pump.
- Raise your pump a little off the bottom of the pond to minimize clogging. If your pump doesn't have feet, a brick will probably do.
- Don't treat your water if you want to keep it safe for pets. Our dog will likely drink from the fountain.
- Don't let it sit stagnant. Fresh standing water is a favorite place for mosquitoes to develop their larvae.

DIY Concrete Stepping Stone Fossil

By CHENG Concrete
(http://www.instructables.com/
id/DIY-CONCRETE-Stepping-
Stone-Fossil/)

In this Instructable, you'll learn a very quick and easy way to make your own concrete fossil (leaf impression). Leaf impressions can be nice details in larger-scale concrete work, or you can follow these instructions as-is to make stepping stones for the backyard or garden. If you have a big project to pour, this is something easy for the kids to play around with, and it keeps any leftover concrete from going to waste.

Difficulty Level: Beginner.

Materials
- Fresh leaf
- Modeling clay
- Smooth, flat, waterproof surface (a scrap piece of ¾" melamine was used, but thick plastic will work, too)
- Sacked concrete
- CHENG Outdoor Pro-Formula Mix

Tools/Supplies
- Spray adhesive
- Diamond sanding pads/sandpaper
- Plastic bag to cover while curing

Concrete Mixing
- Bucket
- Water
- Particle mask
- Rubber gloves

Step 1: Make Clay Wall

Clean up the surface you'll be casting on with denatured alcohol. Any dirt, scratches, imperfections, and texture will be visible in the finished piece of concrete.

For a very smooth finish, you might try casting on a piece of glass or acrylic. Any surface that won't absorb water will work. If you want to use something like wood, it has to be sealed first or the wood will take the moisture out of the concrete and the surface will be clouded and rough.

115

Roll out a few "snakes" and form up the walls by pinching the clay between your fingers and pressing down. It's important that the clay has a good bond to the casting surface. This technique will only work with relatively short walls—anything too tall and the pressure of the concrete will cause the walls to blow out.

great *Sequoia sempervirens* that thrives behind the concrete workshop here in wonderful Berkeley, California. Try using leaves from the backyard, a local park, or your favorite forest. Part of what makes this project fun is foraging for leaves and exploring along the way.

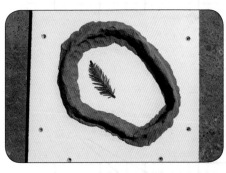

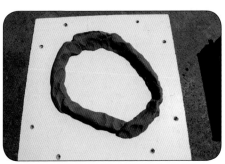

Step 2: Glue Leaf to Base

Liberally spray the "back" of the leaf with spray adhesive, wait a few minutes for it to get tacky, and then press it down somewhere inside the clay wall. Don't spray the adhesive directly on the casting surface—it will leave a rough texture.

Try to pour the concrete as soon as possible after the leaf is stuck down. The longer you wait, the more likely the leaf will begin to peel up. Avoid using dry leaves because they will suck moisture from the concrete. I used one in this example but would have had better results with a fresh leaf.

Some leaves will give a better impression than others, so just experiment. The leaf used here is from a

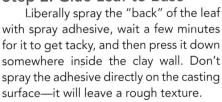

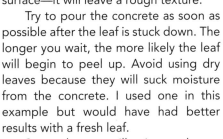

Step 3: Mix, Pour, and Vibrate Concrete

Mix up some concrete! I added CHENG Outdoor Pro-Formula to Sakrete 5000+ bagged concrete. Outdoor Pro-Formula is an ad-mixture that contains pigment (comes in six colors), water reducer, and is air-entrained to help it stand up to the freeze/thaw cycle outdoors.

backyard

Press the edges of the leaf down one last time before pouring concrete in the form. If the concrete seeps under the edge of the leaf, you might only get half of a leaf impression.

Take a handful of concrete and drop it into the form. Smear it around the casting surface (this will help minimize air bubbles on that surface) but don't hit the leaf. Be careful not to bump the clay walls in the process, and try not to over-fill the form.

Vibrate the concrete by pounding on the table and by gently dropping one edge of the base down on the tabletop from a few inches (this is called drop compaction). When the air bubbles come to the surface, wipe across them so they pop and smooth out the top surface as much as you can.

Step 4: Cover and Cure

Cover the concrete with painter's plastic or a plastic bag. Place the form on a level surface, *not* in direct sunlight, to cure for three or four days. You can always add Rapid Set to your concrete mix if you want to de-mold your pieces the next day.

Step 5: Remove Clay Walls

Pry the clay walls back with your fingers and peel them away. The clay can be re-used, so try to remove any pieces of concrete. The concrete piece should come loose from the casting surface at this point.

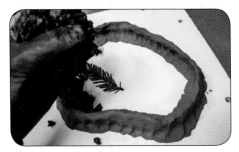

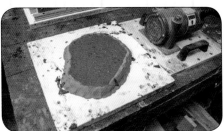

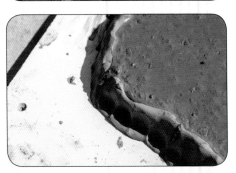

backyard

Step 6: Remove Leaf

Now is the tedious step of removing the leaf from the concrete. The grey area around the leaf is the result of the leaf sucking up moisture. Using a fresh leaf will solve this problem. Use a knife, razor blade, or push pin to remove the old leaf. You're actually breaking away thin pieces of concrete and digging out the leaf below. Work deliberately and patiently like any good archaeologist.

Step 7: Sand and Finish

Sand any rough edges with diamond sanding pads or sandpaper. Diamond pads will be more effective, but sandpaper can work too. The finished concrete can be ground, polished, and then protected with CHENG Sealer and Wax.

Using clay to build form walls does have some limitations beyond a small project like this, but it gives a range of freedom that you don't normally find in concrete formwork. Have a few forms ready to pour at the same time and with just a little bit of work you'll quickly be on your way to making a unique garden pathway.

Section 4

Accessories

Paracord Bracelet with a Side Release Buckle

By Stormdrain
(http://www.instructables.com/
id/Paracord-bracelet-with-a-side-
release-buckle/)

This tutorial will show how to make a paracord bracelet with a side release buckle. When made on a larger scale, you can make this for use as a dog or cat collar as well. A reliable online source for paracord is the Supply Captain; for side release buckles, check out Creative Designworks.

Step 1: Materials
- Paracord or equivalent ⅛" diameter cord
- A tape measure or ruler
- Scissors
- Side release buckle
- A lighter (torch lighter works best)

The amount of cord used can vary, but for this example, we'll use 10' of paracord to start with. Actual amount of cord used for the bracelet is about 1' of cord for every 1' of knotted bracelet length. So if your wrist is 8", you'd use approximately 8' of cord.

Step 2: Measure Wrist
Wrap the paracord around you wrist and make a note of where the cord meets. Hold this point next to your ruler or tape measure and that's your wrist size.

121

Step 3: Find the Center of the Cord

Hold the ends of the cord together and find the center of the loop. Take the center of the cord and pull it through one end of the buckle (either side of the buckle, it doesn't matter). Now pull the cord ends through the loop until it's tightened up and attached to the buckle.

Step 4: Finding the Bracelet Length

Take the buckle apart and pull the free ends of the cord through the other part of the buckle, sliding it up towards the attached part. You're going to measure the distance between the two buckle ends for the bracelet size for your wrist. Add about 1" to your measured wrist length—this will make the finished bracelet a comfortable fit.

You're measuring from the end of the female part of the buckle to the flat part of the male end of the buckle. (The part with the prongs doesn't count for the measurement because the prongs fit inside the female part of the buckle when the bracelet is closed.)

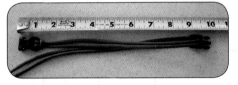

Step 5: Start Making the Knots

The knot used for the bracelet has a few different names—cobra stitch, Solomon bar, and Portuguese sinnet. Take the cord on the left side and place it under the center strands running between the buckle ends. Now take the cord on the right side under the left side cord, over the center strands, and through the loop of the left side cord. Tighten up the cords so the half knot you just formed is next to the buckle. Now take the right side cord under the center strands. The left side cord goes under the right side cord, over the center strands, and thru the loop of the right side cord. Tighten up the cords (not too tight, just until they meet the resistance of the knot) and now you have a completed knot. You will continue doing this, alternating the left and right sides as you go. If you don't alternate, you'll quickly see a twisting of the knots; just undo the last knot and alternate it to correct.

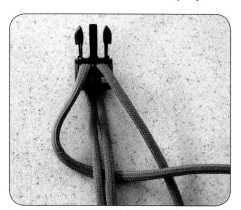

Step 6: Continue knotting

Keep tying the knots until you have filled the space between the buckle ends. The knots should be uniform from one end to the other. Tie each knot with the same tension to keep them all the same size.

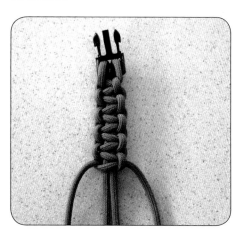

Step 7: Trim the Excess Cord and Melt the Ends

You can now use your scissors to trim off the extra cord closely to the last knot you tied. I trim one at a time, and use my lighter to quickly melt the end I cut, wait a second for the melted cord to cool just a bit and then use my thumb to press the melted end onto the surrounding cord so it hardens as it attaches. You must be careful with this step. The melted cord is extremely hot, and it's possible to get burned, so you might also try using a soldering iron or wood burning tool for the melting step if you wish, or even use something like a butter knife or the knurled section of a tool to flatten out the melted end of the cord to finish it.

123

An alternative to melting the ends is to tuck/pull the ends under the last couple of knots. I have used hemostats to do this on the inside of the bracelet then trimmed them to finish. It does work and is just barely noticeable as the cords add a slight bulge at that end of the bracelet.

Step 8: You're Finished

If you did everything correctly, it should look something like the finished one below. Once you know what you're doing, you can vary the amount of cord used by making the knots tighter or looser and pushing the knots closer together as you go can use more cord.

A tip for paracord bracelets: If the side release buckle is large enough, you can loop the paracord around them again before you start knotting, to fill in the extra room on the buckle. The ½" side release buckles are a tight fit for this but will work, and the ⅝" size are just right. This leaves a two-strand core for the bracelet when you start knotting. Now, you could also have a four strand core by starting with a lark's head on the first buckle end, using a double wrap on the second buckle end (at your wrist size), running the cord back to and over the first buckle end, then knotting over the four-strand core.

Or, for a six strand-core, lark's head first buckle, run the two strands around the second buckle (at your wrist size), back to and around the first buckle (now has four strands around), then back to and around the second buckle, and start knotting around the six core strands. This gives extra cord in case you need it for whatever, but it also makes the paracord bracelets thicker and more rounded, which I personally didn't care for.

Step 9: Other Variations

Once you have the hang of the basic bracelet/collar, you can add another layer of cobra stitches overlapping first set of knots, called a king cobra stitch/doubled Solomon bar/doubled Portuguese sinnet. The amount of cord used for a king cobra is about twice as much as for the regular stitch. Glow-in-the-dark cord can be found at CoolGlowStuff.com. Both the $\frac{1}{16}$" and $\frac{3}{32}$" sizes work well for the bracelets and can be used alone or combined with paracord.

Handyman's Valentine Gift— Screw-Nut Ring Pair

By Taotaoba
(http://www.instructables.com/
id/Handymans-Valentine-gift-
Screw-Nut-rings-pair-/)

Here is a Valentine's Day gift you can make in fifteen minutes. It's a screw and a nut made into a pair of rings. Perfect for DIY-ers and a perfect fit for lovers.

Step 1: What You Need

Materials

- 1 brass screw and nut, #6, available from hardware store
- #14 copper wire, 6" long. I took a ground wire from the #14 cable.

Tools

- Solder iron and solder (avoid Pb, use lead-free solder)
- Vice
- Hacksaw
- Steel wool
- Hammer
- Pliers

Step 2: Make the bands

Bend the copper wire around a steel tube and cut to fit the fingers. Hammer the ends a little bit. Polish with steel wool. Pre-dip with solder for easy assembly later. You need one for you and another one for your significant other.

Step 4: Solder and Done!

Have a look. They fit perfectly. So do you! Happy Valentine's Day!

Step 3: Modify the Nut and Screw

With a hacksaw, cut the screw to around 5mm long. Slot the nut half deep. With a triangle file, file V-shaped slots on both nut and screw head. Predip the V slots.

accessories

Wood Ring
By delno
(http://www.instructables.com/ id/Wood-Ring/)

This Instructable will show you how to make a simple wood ring.

Materials:
- Piece of wood veneer, approximately 6" × 6"
- Wood glue
- Food coloring
- Clear nail polish

Tools:
- Scissors
- Drill
- Band saw
- ⅝" drill bit
- Belt sander or sandpaper

Approximate time: 1 to 2 hours of work and about two nights of drying time for wood glue and dyes.

Step 1: Cutting the Chips

Use heavy-duty scissors to cut chips that are about 1" on both sides. This ring has a thickness of 6 chips, but, depending on the veneer you use and the desired thickness, you can adjust accordingly.

Step 2: Dyeing the Wood

This step is optional. I've made rings in the past without dye. For those, I use a wood burner on low to give the ring a slightly rustic look and polish. That aesthetic is more appealing to me, but I'll include the directions for the colored ring since it is more complicated.

Using a glass dish, mix a strong dye out of water and food coloring and let the chips soak in it overnight. I chose pink and teal for these chips—three of each color. After about eight hours, rinse the chips and let them dry completely.

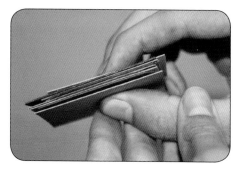

Step 4: Shaping the Ring

Choose a drill bit that is slightly narrower than the diameter of your finger. This will allow you to sand the inside of the ring smooth. I've found that a ⅝" bit generally works for an average finger. Drill a pilot hole, and then the final hole, making sure to leave room around the edges for the ring itself.

Then, use a band saw to carefully cut out the rough shape of your ring, leaving it slightly larger than desired so that it can be sanded smooth.

Step 3: Making the Ply

These veneers will be glued together to make a very thin, strong plywood. Decide on a design for the ring, based on your colors, alternating the grain of the wood to make the ply stronger. Between each layer of wood, lay down a thin, even layer of wood glue, then clamp it all in place between two spare pieces of wood.

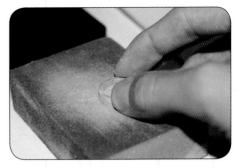

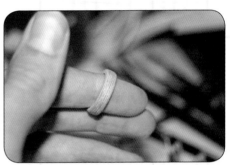

Step 5: Finishing the Ring

Using a belt sander or rough sandpaper, sand the ring to its desired shape and size. The ply is quite strong, so don't worry too much about keeping it thick for strength's sake. Then hand-sand the ring using a fine sandpaper (something around 400 should be the last sanding). Now finish the ring. The finish should offer an aesthetic as well as functional purpose. For the colored ring, I liked something clear and shiny, so I used a hard clear nail polish. For the non-colored ring, this is when I would lightly burn the wood.

Step 6: Finished Ring

Once the finish is dry, the ring is done!

Section 5
Entertain

Have you ever seen those little music boxes you wind up, or crank, that play a little tune over and over from a little metal drum of notes, and wished they did more than play the same ten-second tune over and over for eternity? If only you could change the song and write your own music for it. . . . Now there's an idea.

After a year of design and work, I completed my Re-Programmable Music Box/Mechanical Synthesizer/Organ Grinder Thingy. It has many names, and is 100% non-electric. Just wood, metal, and good ol' people power.

I began this project as a sort of proof-of-concept, designing something from scratch without a lot to base it off of, and a whole lot of engineering problems to solve. Also, I didn't really know what I was doing. It was intended to be a learning and problem-solving experience. And it was a lot of fun.

Step 1: Design and Planning

Since I was starting this project entirely from scratch, I needed to make a flawless design that could be easily worked with, and a good design always reduces waste. I decided to use oak and, at $60 per a 10' plank, I didn't want to waste any. Also, it's pretty complex and precision is extremely important for everything to work correctly.

entertain

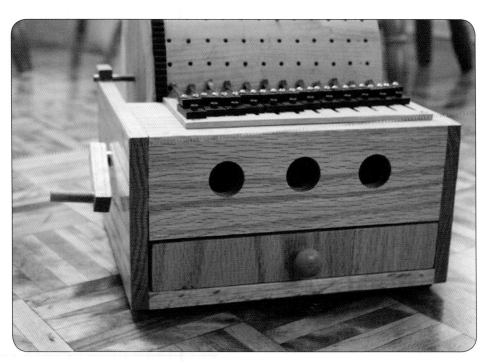

I started with this idea: a large wooden cylinder will hold metal pegs. It will rotate and force the pegs to pluck metal tines, which are tuned to specific notes.

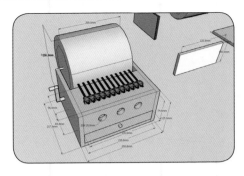

I selected twelve notes across, since it seemed like a very flexible number of notes and allowed me to fill it with a simple eight-note scale in the middle, with a few extra high and low notes. I could also tune in flats or sharps, if I wanted some specifically, or get almost all of a chromatic scale in. I selected thirty-two notes "around" the cylinder, because that's what you need to play Pop Goes The Weasel, or any eight-bar song using quarter notes.

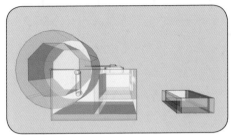

The cylinder is made of softwood, 8" in diameter, that I picked up from a nearby carpenter for free. I found a belt that fit snugly around it to use along with a few gears and a belt for the cranking mechanism.

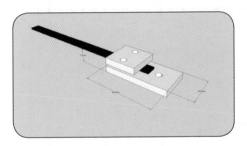

The tine material was cut from the prongs of a garden rake. This works great because it is flexible but snaps right back into place. The tine holder design was sort of up in the air until the rest of the machine was done, so that I could do testing. Initial designs were too complex and tiny, but the final design is about as simple as possible, I believe.

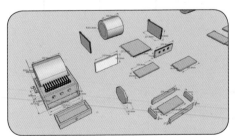

Originally I wanted to use almost all wood for this project, but it turned out wood wasn't going to offer the precision that I needed for the tines. I ended up doing it with a CNC at my college. In Step 7, I hypothesize how it could be accomplished without such expensive tools.

When designing the wooden frame, try to place the pieces to get as few exposed edges as possible. For the edges you do have, try to align them so that they create borders and still look appealing to the eye.

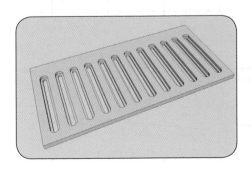

Step 2: Materials and Tools

Materials:

- Oak plank (10' long × 8" wide × ¾" thick is what I started with)
- 8" long × 8" diameter wood cylinder
- Aluminum plate
- 1" wide ¼" thick aluminum stock
- 100 steel pegs
- 384⅛" diameter × ⅛" long magnets
- Rake tines
- 8" rubber belt
- Smaller belt
- 3 gears
- Carriage bolt and nut
- ~12" long ¼" steel rod
- ¼" wooden dowel
- Biscuits
- Instrument mallet

Tools:

- Table saw
- Band saw
- Drill press
- Number drill set
- Fractional drill set
- Wood glue
- Clamps
- Drill bits
- Biscuit cutter
- Planer
- 1" hole saw
- Polyurethane wood sealant
- Pliers

Note: I'm going to assume you know how to use your planer, your table saw, your band saw, your drill press, etc., and I won't go into detail about the operation of the machines. If you're using someone else's machines, have

them teach you how to use them and have someone around for safety.

Step 3: Woodwork—Part 1

So it's tough to find wood in the shapes you want at the lumber store, so I bought a 10' long piece that was only 8" wide. My solution was to chop it into three 3.3' segments and glue them together to form a 2' × 3.3' oak board.

First, chop the plank into three even pieces. Then, plane them down to ½" thickness, since ¾" is too thick for such a small project. Next, cut biscuit notches with the biscuit cutter and glue them in place. Be sure to mark the locations of the biscuits so that you can plan around them, so they won't be visible after making cuts. Clamp it together and let it dry for twenty-four hours.

Measure the circumference of the cylinder, and divide it by thirty-two. Mark thirty-two lines all the way around the cylinder. Now, mark twelve holes along each line for each note. There should be 384 points to drill now.

To drill the cylinder, set a vice on the drill press bed and put a few rags inside the open jaws so that the wood won't get damaged. Use a weight on a string to check that the line of holes you are drilling are straight and vertical. Find a number drill that is a few thousandths of an inch larger than ⅛" and drill the holes exactly 1" deep using the depth control on the press.

Next, glue a magnet into the bottom of each hole. This is to prevent the pegs from falling out when the drum holds them upside down. The best way to do this is to place a magnet on the end of a steel peg, put a drop of glue on it, and carefully push it down into the hole. It should protrude from the hole by $\frac{1}{8}$". Then, tap it lightly with a hammer to make sure it's in proper contact at the bottom.

Step 4: Woodwork—Part 2

Hop back on the computer and devise a means to get your shape dimensions onto paper. You can export 2D images from your design software and print them to-scale, or you can just read off dimensions and mark them on the wood with a pencil and a square. When placing things on the wood, remember to keep visible edges away from the biscuits! It helps if your design is on separate cutouts so that you can play with the positioning to maximize wood yield. Remember, the table saw blade will consume about $\frac{1}{8}$" of wood, so leave gaps between your pieces.

I'd like to make a safety note. Table saws are horrible, ridiculously dangerous machines. If you are not incredibly afraid of the saw, then *do not* use it. You need a very healthy amount of fear, so that you'll take every precaution when using it, or you'll lose your thumbs. I'm serious.

Once your pieces are cut, there are a few holes to drill. Drill the holes for the shaft that the drum will rotate on and for the sound-port holes on the front piece. Don't drill the holes in the octagonal pieces that will go in the drum yet, since you'll need to properly find the center once they're in place. Now start clamping and gluing. I'll admit, I was on a tight schedule at the time and had to get these parts done in a few hours, so I cheated and used a nail gun. It was a terrible idea, nail guns cause splits in

hardwood, so don't do it! Take the time to use glue and clamps properly.

To make the crank handle, cut a 1.5" piece of dowel and a 2" piece of dowel. Cut a piece of leftover oak into a 2" × ½" piece. Drill a ¼" deep hole near one end on one side, and another hole at the other end on the opposite side. Glue one dowel into each hole. The 2" dowel will go inside the machine; 2" may be longer than needed so it can be cut down accordingly.

The way I came up with to glue the end pieces into the wooden drum was like this: First, put wood glue around the outside of the first octagon and lay it flat on the table. Then, put the barrel down on top of it so they fit in together. Make sure they're lined up correctly and wipe off any excess or oozing glue. Wait for it to dry. Then take a center-finding tool and locate the center of this side of the drum. Drill a ¼" to meet your shaft diameter. Now, do the same thing with the second octagon, but this time, to make sure everything is pushed flat and the octagon isn't too far into the barrel, push it with a rod or dowel through the hole in the opposite end. Once the glue is dry, find the center of the second side and drill a second hole. Everything should be perfect!

Cut a 12" length of ¼" solid steel rod for the shaft the drum will rotate on. File the ends so they're smooth.

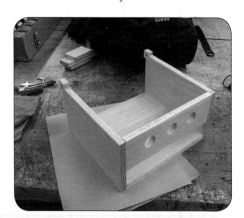

Step 5: Mechanics

Now we need to start working on the mechanical linkages and crank for the drum movement. Since putting the crank right at drum-level would result in the crank hitting the table, I had to devise some transfer mechanisms to allow me to put it higher up.

I found some plastic gears that meshed correctly with the 8" rubber belt I had for the drum. I glued two of the gears together and glued a long bolt into a hole I drilled through the side of the box. On the end of the box, I drilled a hole and glued a nut into it. This would let me insert a machine screw with a captive armature on it, which held a gear on the end. This would in turn let me tension a transfer belt to prevent slipping of the belts and gears but still make the crank easy to turn.

The result was what you see in the image. The system works pretty well, and I don't think there could be a much easier way to do it without fabricating custom gears.

An important thing to think about is the space you have. There was only about 1"of clearance between the internal wall and the drum, so space was tight.

Step 6: Finishing the Wood

I decided to finish most of the wood early, because I wasn't going to be able to keep working on the project for the next four months, and I didn't want it to get dirty or change shape from water in the air. I just coated it with a few layers of Minwax Polyurethane to make it shiny and bring out the color of the wood a little bit more.

After the polyurethane is dry, squeeze the 8" belt onto the edge of the drum. I cut the belt in half because it was too wide and covered the first row of holes. If it doesn't hold in place by friction alone, you can use finishing nails to tack it in place.

Step 7: The Musical Mechanics

This was a major engineering challenge for quite a while. I had a few designs that were a bust; they were just far too small to be practical. I ended up distilling the ideas into what I think is as simple as could be possible.

The tine, which is a piece of steel from a leaf rake, is sandwiched between two aluminum plates. The tine is kinked at the tip and is roughly the length it needs to be, plus enough length to be held in the plates firmly. This is secured with two small screws that pass through the top plate and into threaded holes in the bottom plate. The bottom plate then sits atop a large aluminum plate with slots machined in it. On the bottom are larger slots with captive nuts in them, held in place against the top of the music box. A screw passes through a hole in the second plate and into one of the nuts so that its position can be controlled by sliding it up and down in the slot. Using this method, the tine length can be tuned to the appropriate note, and then the tine holder can be moved towards the pins on the barrel and lined up for just the right amount of plucking force.

To build the tine holders, I used 1" wide ¼" thick aluminum stock. Since I only had ⅗" of space per tine, I cut the pieces down to 0.59", and then into 0.59" and 1.18" long segments.

The tines can be cut from the rake using a hack saw or angle grinder. Cutting their lengths is a hit-or-miss guessing game, however. Depending on their width, thickness, and composition, their resonating characteristics will change greatly, so I can't give a list of predetermined lengths. You'll have to just cut a few and experiment to find what works for your tines. The tips can be bent with two pairs of pliers.

I used a CNC to cut the aluminum plate. Now, I know that using a CNC is out of the realm of 99% of readers, but I had the resources and it was the best logical way to do the design I had created. If it had to be done using simple tools, I would say sandwich pieces of wood together to form the slots, or use a chisel to carve out the slots for the

nuts and a drill and needle files to do the rest.

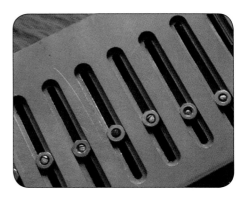

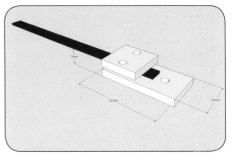

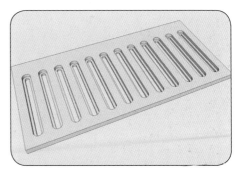

Step 8: Final Assembly and Tuning

Tuning is a pain-staking process that takes an hour or two. The tines can be tuned to lots of different scales, but I selected a simple set of notes from the piano. They are:

- A3
- B3
- C4 (middle C)
- D4
- E4
- F4
- G4
- A4
- B4
- C5
- D5
- E5

The result is a pretty good range of notes that works for lots of little songs, like "Mary Had A Little Lamb," "Hot Cross Buns," and "Pop Goes The Weasel."

To tune, start by arranging all the tines by length, and then place them tightly in the tine holders. Mount all the holders on the aluminum plate, but not near the drum. Tighten them down so they will resonate nicely. Using a piano or a virtual piano (like http://www.virtualpiano.net/), play the note that you want to tune to. Strike the corresponding tine with a plastic mallet. If it is too high, loosen the two screws holding the tine and wiggle the tine out further. If it is too low, push it in further. Once the notes sound right (and you'll know when), you can tighten down the tine as tightly as possible so it can't slip. Then, slide the tine holder up to the drum and put a peg right near it. You want the peg to just barely touch the tine as it comes up and then pluck it. You don't want the tine to bend upwards more than a few millimeters. Too much force could break the tines over time or cause the gears and belts to slip.

Repeat this process until all the tines are tuned. Set up a "test pattern" by placing pegs in diagonal lines across the drum, so it will play the scale when rotated. Test it out! If it sounds good, try out a song or two. You should be able to use music written for a recorder—that should work well on this machine. Chords are possible, but elaborate ones may require more torque to pluck than the crank will allow.

never be achieved with wood. If I were to ever try and build something like this again, it would have to be made entirely from metal. Other than that, I don't think the design has any major flaws.

Step 9: Improvements and Considerations

I'll admit, after all the time and effort I put into good design on this project, it didn't turn out as well as I had hoped. Part of the problem is the insane precision required to do this properly, which could

Birch Bark Flask

By Jeremy Ashby (wizworm)
(http://www.instructables.com/
id/Birch-Bark-Flask/)

Create a flask out of paper birch bark!

Step 1: Peel the Bark from Your Victim

Use a sharp box cutter to score the bark in a long straight line down the stick. Use a knife to slowly separate the bark from the branch. Then, scrape any leftover material off the bark with the knife.

Step 2: Make the Top and Bottom

Use a Sawzall or hand saw to cut discs off of the end of the branch. Cut 2.5" discs for the top and bottom of the flask. Cut one 1.5" disk for the plug. I used a hatchet to break up the plug piece to larger than the finished size. I whittled the plug down to size using my knife. (Be safe here and don't cut your hand.) You could start with a dowel here and whittle it down to make it look "handmade." Drill a hole in the top disc to hold the finished plug. (You could dispense with the top and make a pen cup for your desk or a drink holder; it would be a posh Starbucks caddy.)

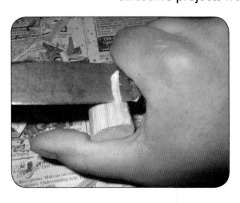

Step 4: Make your Own Nails to Attach the Top and Bottom

Take a piece of brass brazing wire that is the thickness of a normal finishing nail; hold it securely in a pair of vise grips. Place the pliers somewhere firm and peen the end with a ball peen hammer. Use light taps to slowly mushroom the end into the head of your new nail. Use side cutters to cut the wire at an angle, creating an off-center point in the tip of the nail to help it drive into the wood. I recommend inserting each nail as you make it, and make sure you make the nail long enough. (I kept dropping them.)

Step 3: Soften and Sew Up the Seam

Place the bark over a steaming sauce pot of water, which will soften it making it easier to bend. Use a large needle (Glovers, sail, etc.) to stitch up the cut side. I used a natural hay bailing twine and striped off a few fibers, softened them in the boiling water, twisted them, and went to town sewing. When finished, insert the top and bottom (sand/file as necessary or apply some more steam to soften the bark).

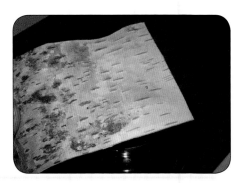

Step 5: Attach Top and Bottom with Newly Made Nails

I used five nails on the top and bottom each, one next to each side of the seam, and three others evenly dispersed. Use your box knife to trim any bark that hangs over the top and bottom. The bottom of the flask did split on me at the end, so I would consider using a hard wood next time. (I'll glue from the inside to "fix this problem.") I also don't think I'd use my own nails on a future version of this project. Also, I could have pre-drilled some of the finished nail holes to ensure a tight fit. Since I will be carrying this around in a leather pouch, I might consider an oval shape that would more easily contour with the other bag contents.

entertain

Build an Inexpensive Cigar Box Guitar at Home

By nickdrj

(http://www.instructables.com/id/Build-an-Inexpensive-Cigar-Box-Guitar-at-Home/)

As a birthday present for my brother, I decided to make him a nice cigar box guitar. This is the first one I've ever made so it was a bit of a learning experience.

Before making the guitar, I decided that it should be made from either found or very cheaply obtained materials. Most of the items I used were not originally meant for use in a guitar. I don't think I spent more than $50 for all the parts. It's not a dirt cheap guitar, but it won't hurt the wallet either.

Also, since I don't have any big power tools, I had to be able to make it in my kitchen using the handheld tools I already had (with the exception of the fingerboard, which I had cut for me from a scrap of plywood at a hardware store).

And lastly, I wanted to make this Instructable because I wanted to share everything I learned, plus to give back for all the helpful guides I used for this project. This project has a lot of steps, so I tried to divide it up in to logical sections.

Tools
- Dremmel (best tool ever)
- Different sandpapers
- Couple of different files
- Coping saw
- Drill
- A lot of clamps
- Hot glue
- Epoxy

Step 1: The Body

The cigar box! I found this nice box at a cigar shop that sells them for $2. (I'm paying for garbage!) It's important to find a box you really like; it will make your guitar stand out! I liked this one because it had rounded sides, which made it really uncommon.

Since the neck will be glued to the top of the box lid, I first made a cut where the neck will go through. I cut it down with a saw and then filed it down. Next I wanted two circular sound holes on either side of the guitar; this way, I can run the neck all the way down the body. I also wanted to make the rims of the sound holes be metal. So I found a nice chrome metal pipe at Home Depot that had nice rims at the end. I cut those off with my coping saw.

I also want the option of this guitar being played electrically, so I will install a piezo pickup in a later step. But I have to make a hole for the mono jack. Since the jack is pretty short, I had to grind down the inside of the box where the jack will be installed. Check the pictures for what I mean.

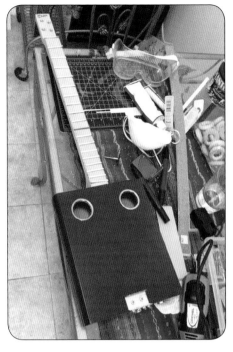

Step 2: The Neck

The neck basically will take up 90 percent of your time. I wanted it to be nice and round at the back, have a base where it connects to the body (much like an acoustic), and be fretted. For the structure, I wanted to keep it simple and run the neck along the whole body, eventually gluing it to the top of the cigar box.

First things first: I cut the neck to the desired length. I didn't use any conventional length, I just picked it intuitively, whatever felt right. Then I cut the hole in the box where the neck will be glued. This gives me an idea where to add the base.

After cutting the neck, I started to work on the heel at the bottom of the neck. I cut out two pieces of wood about 4″ long from the remaining neck wood. I glued them together using Titebond wood glue. Using a clamp, I pressed them together and let it dry for thirty minutes. Then I glued the two pieces onto the main neck board.

entertain

147

Next, I cut the glued heel to the desired profile with my coping saw. Finally, I shaped it using a file.

Step 3: The Head

I wanted the head of the guitar to be slightly recessed so that the strings get more tension. First, I glued another piece of wood to the back of the head. I cut it from the same wood as the neck, and then cut it in half, so that it was about ¼" thick. Then I grinded it down with a file to make it nice and curved. Next I cut ¼" off the front of the head. Then I filed everything down to make it as smooth as I could get it. After that, I did my best to guess where to put the holes for the tuner. I then drilled them. I don't have power tools so it got a little splintery around the edges. No big deal though, it gets covered up by the tuners. Lastly, I put in a decal at the top. I put my brother's name. I used a technique where I printed it in reverse on acetate then glued it on with photo mount. Then later, when I apply the finish, it gets sealed. Since the neck and head is complete, I smoothed out the back with a file to make it nice and round.

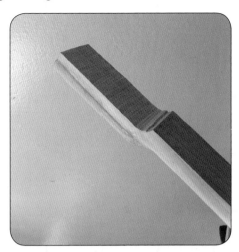

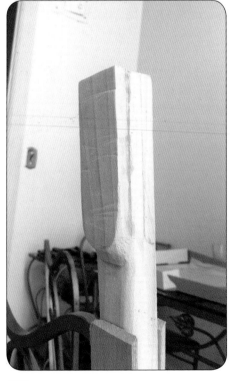

entertain

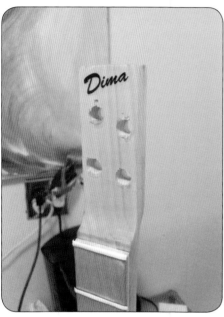

strings using the Dremel. Lastly, I drilled a couple of holes at the bottom and screwed it into the body of the guitar.

Step 4: The Bridge

The bridge I made in two parts. First, to hold the strings in place, I used a heavy duty picture hanger I got at Home Depot (sawing off the peg that is used for hanging). I used a large screw to keep it in place. The screw went through the cigar box and into the piece of wood for the neck, making it a pretty solid fit. Then, in the trash I found a handle that was attached to a drawer that had been thrown away. This turned out to be perfect for the saddle—it just needed some shaping. I chopped off the sides and cut it down a bit so the action wasn't so high. Then I added notches for the

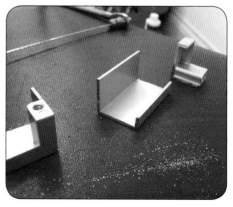

hanger. I cut up the wire using big wire cutters (later a Dremel—so much easier). Make sure to cut them a little long—you will grind them down to shape. I then glued on the very top fret using epoxy.

At this point, I measured very accurately the distance from the top fret to the bridge. This is very important as it will determine the spacing of the fret. Then I went to stewmac.com. They have a very good fret calculator. I inserted the length of the scale and how many frets I wanted. Using the measurements stewmac.com provided, I penciled them all in one by one. Remember to always measure from the top fret; don't measure fret to fret, because it is easier to make a mistake and screw up the notes. After penciling them in, I used a coping saw to saw little gutters for the frets. You may need to go into them using a file as well.

When done, you can glue the frets into place using epoxy. Use a piece of wood and clamps to hold the frets in place while the glue dries. Once they are glued solidly, cut the edges off using a Dremel with a cutting attachment. Wear eye protection—sparks will fly.

Step 5: Fretting

I got a piece of plywood scrap cut to size at a hardware store; it's basically the thickness of the neck. I cut it lengthwise and glued it on to the neck. Keeping with the goal of using found/cheap materials, I decided to use wire cut from a common

Step 6: Fret Dots

I only decided to add fret marks on the side of the neck. To do this, I basically drilled holes on the 3rd, 5th, 7th, 9th, and 12th frets (double holes for 12). Then, I hammered tiny nails into the holes, sawed them off with my Dremel, and filed them down. Easy!

entertain

Step 7: Peizo Pickup

The Piezo pickup is a really easy way to get any acoustic guitar to play electrically. The one thing I'd recommend is getting one that is easy to disassemble, so you can get the metal plate that acts as the mic out. The one I got from RadioShack was sealed shut, and I had to grind up the plastic to get to the piezo element inside. After removing it, I soldered two wires to the yellow ones that came with the piezo element. Then I coiled them together.

Inside the box, I added loop screws to run the wire and soldered it to the mono jack I installed earlier. I installed the piezo element using a bit of hot glue from a glue gun to raise it above the wood.

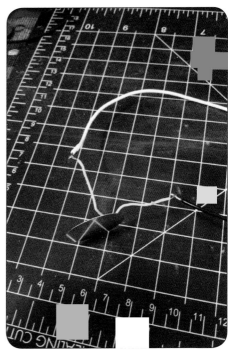

entertain

Step 8: Applying the Finish

Applying the finish to the neck is pretty straightforward. I used a clear lacquer for the job. I covered the frets up with some masking tape, so that they wouldn't get all sticky. I know I'm probably doing this backwards, but it is what it is . . . I applied a coat and waited about an hour. Once it was dry, I used a fine sandpaper to smooth it out. Then, I repeated a couple of more times. And that's it.

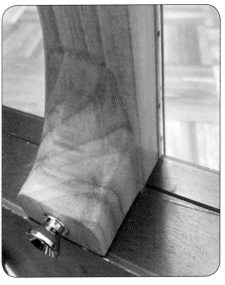

Step 9: Finished!

And here is the finished guitar. It wasn't too difficult to make, just a bit time consuming. It was a great learning experience. I hope to improve on it in the next one. And I hope it helps anyone else making these fun DIY instruments.

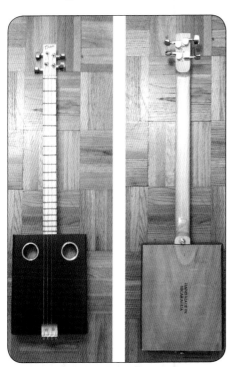

entertain

Wooden Beer Bottle Crate

By Kevin P. Verratti

(pubcrawlingpb)

http://www.instructables.com/id/
Wooden-Beer-Bottle-Crate/

I play for the scenario paintball team Pub Crawling. We have more than twenty members on the team and, with a name like Pub Crawling, it should be obvious that we drink a lot of malted beverages after our games. We travel all over the United States to play paintball and have traveled to Scotland and England for events. To keep up our supply of beverages and meet the demands of the team, several members have begun home brewing beer. Naturally, bringing a full keg setup for after the game isn't always a reality, and sometimes I just want to have a few beers put in long term storage to try my hand at aging them. Though, for the most part, aging beers is more a matter of testing my patience.

What I really wanted was something that was fully enclosed, and something that wouldn't have a lid that would come open if it tipped over or rolled around in the back of a truck or trailer without anyone noticing. Also it had to have dividers for the bottles, and I didn't want it to weight a ton or cost an arm and a leg.

I looked around for plans to make wooden bottle crates to hold beer and couldn't really find what I was after. So I incorporated a few of the best ideas that met my needs from all of them and this is what I came up with.

Tools:
- Table saw (though a radial arm saw or skill saw could do it, too)
- Drill

Material:
- 1 1" × 12" × 8' Pine Board $10
- 2 2' × 2' × ¼" birch panel $10
- Glue
- Screws
- ⅜" hemp rope

Assuming you have some rope, glue, and screws on hand, $20 is enough to make two crates with very little waste wood left over. These crates each hold twelve bottles, are sturdy enough to take a beating, and yet aren't so heavy that one person can't carry two of them at the same time. I will also add that I am nowhere near good enough a woodworker to make anything super precise like cabinets or 90° angles. So if I can make these crates, so can you. It took me about three hours to make two crates, including the time it took to take all these pictures, too. I'm sure someone who has even the slightest clue of what they are doing could make them even faster.

Step 1: Cutting Grooves for Top and Bottom

The first step is to cut the grooves for the top and bottom panels. Using a dado blade in my table saw, I set the groove to start at a ½" from the edge of the board and to be roughly ¼" deep.

I ran the board through twice so that there was a groove for both the tops and bottoms. I actually chose to use the nicer side of the board as the inside and used the really knotted, pitted, and banged up side as the outside. People spend a lot of time trying to stress a board to make it look rustic; I chose boards that were pre-rustic-ed.

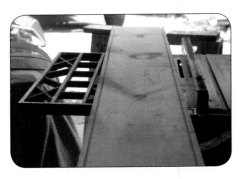

Step 2: Change Blades

Now take out the dado blade set and swap over to a standard combination blade, rip/cross blade, or cross cut blade. It is worth the extra $5 to get a carbide tipped blade. They last so much longer than a plane steel blade that you'll make that $5 back in no time. A good combination blade really is worth the extra couple of dollars.

Step 3: Cut the Board in Half

Cut the board roughly in half. Remember when I said that this project has enough materials to make two crates? Cutting the board in half will just make it easier to wield and will make our cuts later. I actually cut this board about 9" shorter than half, but I knew my overall dimensions were not more than 42" long.

Step 4: Cut the Sides

Now we need to cut the sides. First, make four boards that are 12" long—these are the long sides. Then cut four boards that are 8⅜"—these are the short sides. There should be about a 10" or so piece of scrap left if you cut the board all at once. This could in theory be used for a third box depending on how much lumber you have.

Step 5: Cutting the Tops and Bottoms

Now, take a piece of the ¼" panel and cut it 9" wide. Do this twice so that you have two strips of panel that are 9" wide × 24" long. This will leave you with one strip that is roughly 6" wide. Hang on to this piece of scrap for later.

Take the two 9" wide sections and cut a piece that is 11.5" long out of each of them. The 11.5" piece is the bottom of your box and the 12.5" piece is the top.

Step 6: Dry Fit

This is a good time to take the panel and do a dry fit to make sure everything works right. You can trim up any pieces that weren't cut deep enough or aren't quite square before adding glue. Once you glue it together, there isn't any going back, so test fitting makes sense.

Step 7: Cut the Door Slide

The top door of the box slides in the grooves at the top of the box. In order to do this, you need to cut the dado groove off from one side of the short wall section. This will leave the perfect spacing for the top to slide in and provide a bit of friction to stop it from sliding out on its own.

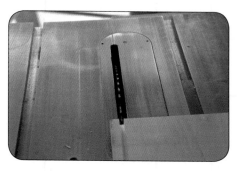

Step 8: Glue and Clamp

Add some glue to the bottom grooves only and put the box together. Hold everything in place with a clamp or two until the glue dries. I put a couple of screws in the box to help hold it in place. I like to pre-drill the screw holes when they are close to the edge to stop the wood from splitting.

Step 9: Cut the Inserts

While the glue is drying, it is a good time to cut the inserts to separate the bottles. Take the 6" piece of left over panel and cut it into two pieces that are 10.5" long. Now take the second piece of 2' × 2' panel and cut it into strips that are 6" wide or equal to the width of the piece of scrap panel. Odds are that it isn't exactly 6" depending on the kerf width of your blade; it could be as narrow as 5.25". Just measure the scrap and make strips from the full panel the same width.

After you have your strips of panel cut, make two more of them 10.5" long. Cut the remainder of the strips so that they are 8⅜" long. These may need to be a tad short at 8⁵⁄₁₆" depending on kerf width and exact internal dimensions of your box.

In the end you should have four pieces that are roughly 6" × 10.5" and six pieces that are 6" × 8⅜".

Step 10: Cut the Tabs

Now you need to cut the tabs. These will interlock and create the pockets to hold each bottle. To do this quickly and easily, put the dado set back on the table saw.

The 10.5" sections will need three cuts. The first cut is in the center of the piece, and the other two cuts are centered between that cut and each end of the board. This means a cut roughly every 2.75" depending on the overall length. The shorter 8⅜" pieces only need two cuts. Each cut will be roughly 2.75" from the end.

There is a little bit of play room in this, as the thickness of the board and the overall internal dimensions of your box could vary depending how precise you are. Your kerf width comes into play a lot here as well. Each cut will be just slightly more than half the depth of the board. In this example, each cut is just over 3" long. You can test out if your cut is deep enough by interlocking the pieces to see if they fit flush. If they aren't flush, you need to cut them a bit longer.

Step 11: Dry Fit the Divider

Now assemble the divider by interlocking the tabs. If everything lined up right, you should be able to put a beer bottle into any section and it will slide right in. Don't worry if one or two of them are a little tight.

Now put the dividers into the box and fill all of the spots. If a couple of the spots are too tight to fit a bottle, do not try to force it. Instead take the divider out and widen the interlocking slot a little bit. This should give the dividers just enough play to snugly hold the bottles.

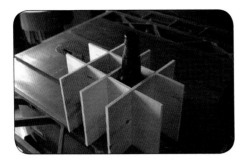

Step 12: Drill Cover

Take the cover pieces and drill a finger hole in them. Anything larger than a 1" hole should do. Try to line the hole up over the dividers; this will stop a beer bottle from trying to fit through the hole should the crate get overturned.

Step 14: Add Beer and Store

You should now have two wooden crates to store twenty-four bottles of beer in. You can also stain/paint/laser engrave/carve whatever you want into these boxes.

Step 13: Add Rope Handles

Now take your drill and make two holes on either side of the short sides of the box. I used a ⅜" drill and made the holes 3.75" from the top and 1.75" from the side of the box.

Now take about 20" of the rope and put it through the holes, tie a knot on either end, and pull it tight. These are now the handles for the crate.

entertain

Wooden Beer Mug

By drean
(http://www.instructables.com/
id/wooden-beer-mug/)

This Instructable is for making a big wooden beer mug. I made it 15cm × 22cm. It is not so suitable for drinking beer (pallet wood can be toxic), but it is good for decorative purposes or, like me, as a trash and beer caps bin.

Step 1: Cutting the Wood

For this mug, I used some pallet wood I had laying around. You will need fifteen sticks cut at a length of 22 cm and at an angle of 12°.

Step 2: Tape It

Put the sticks around something round and tape them together, but leave one opening.

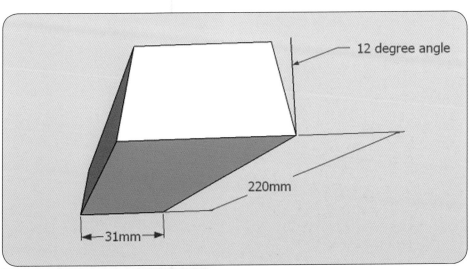

12 degree angle

220mm

31mm

Step 3: Gluing

Now take the whole thing, put it on a flat surface, and put some glue between the sticks.

Step 4: Tourniquet It

Now fold it together again. I used some rope and a pair of screwdrivers to tighten the sticks together. Now you can let the glue dry.

Step 5: The Ear

Now make the ear. Mine is approximately 20cm × 8cm. I did all the sanding with an angle grinder. When the glue of the mug has dried, you can also sand this.

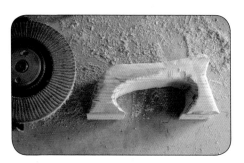

Step 6: Decorating

To make it look better, I've put some rings made out of sheet metal around them. It is best to screw these behind the handle into one piece of wood. You could also use some rope to put around the mug. With the angle grinder, I made some grooves and glued the rings in.

Step 7: Putting It Together

Now put the ear on it. I made the mistake of putting the bottom in before screwing the ear on from the inside. Next, glue the bottom in and do some more sanding.

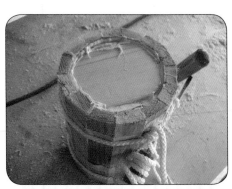

entertain

Section 6

Kitchen

I was disappointed recently to find that there are no Instructables on making wooden bowls with a scroll saw, even though there are lots of books published on the subject. So I've decided to fill the gap.

All you'll need is a scroll saw and a few other tools to get started. I like this project because it minimizes the amount of wasted wood (unlike bowls made with a lathe), and the bowls produced have very interesting designs. It's also surprisingly easy, as long as you have the patience to sand it to perfection.

Step 1: Tools and Materials

Tools
- Scroll saw (mandatory)
- Table saw
- Miter saw
- Planer
- Jointer
- Drill press with adjustable stage (for different angles)
- Belt/disc sander
- Digital caliper/straight edge

Materials
- Wood glue
- Scroll saw blades (they will break often)
- Pen/pencil
- Clamps, clamps, and more clamps
- Sandpaper and sandpaper belts for sanders
- Varnish (and/or stain, depending on what you want to do)
- At least 1' of wood, can be pieces of various woods

Note: If you plan on putting food in the bowl, you should avoid using exotic hardwoods. Many of those woods contain toxic chemicals, which can contaminate food and possibly harm you. However, most domestic hardwoods are fine for use with food.

Step 2: Wood and Laminates

The first step is to prepare the blank from which you will cut the bowl pieces. I recommend making the blank at least 12" × 12". It can be a solid piece of wood or a laminate of several different types of wood. If you use more pieces with contrasting colors, it makes the final design on the bowl much more impressive. I used a parallel laminate of three types of wood for this project, but you can do far more just by changing the thickness of the strips or gluing them together at different angles.

Here are the general steps for making a good laminate:

1. Cut the desired strips to the desired width with a table saw.
2. Use a miter saw to cut the strips to the desired length.
3. Use a jointer to smooth and level the sides of the strips.
4. Fit the pieces together to make sure there are no gaps.

Step 3: Gluing the Laminate

Special care must be taken while gluing the strips of the laminate together to avoid warping. Choose a flat surface that you can use clamps with and clean it. Look ahead to Step 7 before gluing. Apply a good amount of glue to each piece and join them together. Do not glue the middle two pieces together if you want to avoid drilling entry holes, as mentioned in Step 7. Carefully wipe up excess glue. Use long clamps to squeeze the pieces together. Use more clamps to keep the laminate flat on the table/ surface. Wipe up any more excess glue. Let the glue dry for about twenty-four hours at or above 55°F.

Step 4: Finishing the Laminate

I highly recommend using a planer to smooth the laminate and to get rid of any warping that may have occurred during gluing. Once you have smooth surfaces on both sides of the laminate, measure its thickness at multiple points to make sure the piece is even.

Step 5: Choosing Bowl Dimensions

The simplest way to make a bowl is to cut the rings at a 45° angle. That way, the rings are as far apart as the laminate is thick. I recommend the diameter of the inner circle be at least 3".

If you want to try different dimensions to make unique bowls, grab

kitchen

a calculator or open up Excel and follow the steps below:

1. Choose a diameter for the inner circle (should be 3–4"): D, cell A2
2. Measure the maximum length/diameter of the laminate: L, cell B2
3. Measure the thickness of the laminate: T, cell C2
4. Choose an angle to cut: (theta), cell D2
5. Calculate width of each ring: X, cell E2
6. Cut and paste this formula into cell E2: =TAN(RADIANS(D2))*C2
7. Calculate the number of rings (round down): N, cell F2
8. Cut and paste this formula into cell F2: =FLOOR((B2-A2)/(2*E2),1)
9. Calculate the final height of the bowl: H, cell G2
10. Cut and paste this formula into cell G2: =(F2+1)*C2
11. Play around with the cut angle (theta) until you are happy with the final height of the bowl.

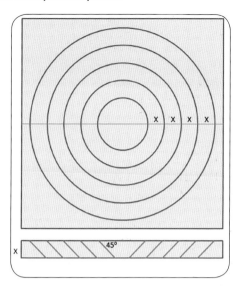

Step 6: Trace the Circles

Once you have calculated the width of each ring (X from last step), you will need to trace the rings onto the bowl, like so:

1. Find the center of the blank and mark it with an X.

	A	B	C	D	E	F	G
1	D	L	T	theta	X	N	H
2	3	12	0.5	45	0.5	9	5
3	inches	inches	inches	degrees	inches	#	inches

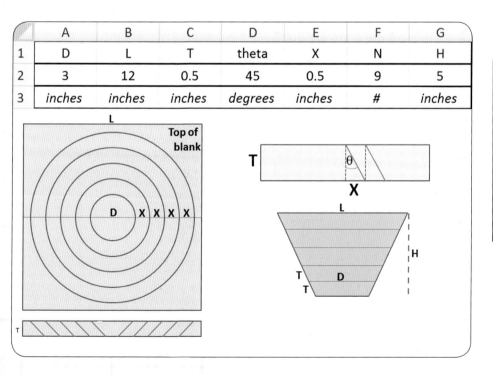

2. Take a stiff piece of card stock (ex: cover of a notebook or holiday card) and cut a 1" wide by 6–12" long strip.
3. On one end of the strip, make a tiny hole with the point of a knife.
4. Draw a straight line from that hole across the length of the strip.
5. Make another hole about "D/2" inches along that line from the first hole.
6. Make more holes, each "X" inches apart, until you've reached the maximum radius of your bowl.
7. Pin the strip down to the blank with a pointy object and carefully trace concentric circles by rotating the strip around the centerpoint on the blank (see below).

angle that will be used to allow you to start cutting. If you have a good drill press and a strong thin bit, you can use this method.

However, I don't have a good drill press, so I can't make consistent entry holes. Therefore, I came up with a way to avoid having to drill them. I simply make the laminate in even halves and cut semi-circles, which are later glued together to give full circles. That way, I don't have to worry about the accuracy of entry holes or putting on/taking off my scroll saw blade. See the second picture below to see exactly what I'm talking about.

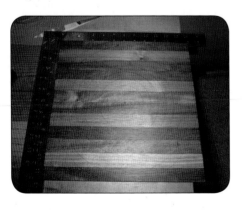

Step 7: Optional: Drilling Entry Holes

Most traditional wood bowls start with a solid piece of wood. To start cutting the rings, entry holes must be drilled with the scroll saw at the same

Step 8: Cutting the Rings

Now it is time to warm up that scroll saw! The method here is pretty self explanatory—just cut the rings out and take your time. Here are some extra pointers:

- Make sure the stage on the scroll saw is adjusted to the proper angle. Cut a test piece and measure the angle, if necessary.
- Go slowly, but never stop moving forward. If you stop or go back, you will remove more wood and scar the bowl.
- Maintain lots of pressure on the piece for a clean, consistent, and quick cut.

Step 9: Glue

Before you do any gluing, mark the pieces so you can glue them together exactly as they were cut. If you forget to do this, some of the bands may not match up properly. If you avoided drilling entry holes, the first thing to do now is to glue the half circles together to make full circles. Use plenty of glue and clamp them down on a flat surface until dry.

Once you have the rings glued, glue them together, one at a time. Make sure that the bands on the outside of the bowl line up as nicely as possible. If you have a spindle sander, don't glue the bottom piece onto the bowl just yet. Leaving the bottom of the bowl open will allow you to easily sand the inside of the bowl using a spindle sander. If you don't have a spindle sander, go ahead and glue the bottom piece.

Put the glued bowl onto a flat surface and compress it with something heavy. Some people use "bowl presses" (Google it), but I just use my old textbooks. Compress the bowl for at least a few hours or until the glue has dried overnight.

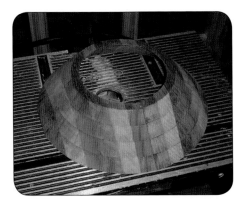

Step 10: Sanding

No matter how good your cuts were, there's a lot of sanding to be done! I prefer a belt sander for this step. I smooth out the outside and inside of the bowl with about 50-grit sand paper, then move up to 120-grit to make it even smoother for finishing. Examine the bowl carefully, rubbing your fingers across the joints to make sure they are as smooth as possible.

I also like to round off the edge of the bowl with my disc sander. Just take your time and evenly sand the edge of the bowl. Be careful not to lose control—disc sanders can quickly gouge your bowl.

Finally, I like to thoroughly sand the inside and outside of the bowl with 120-grit sandpaper to get any small spots the belt sander may have missed.

kitchen

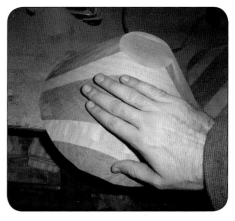

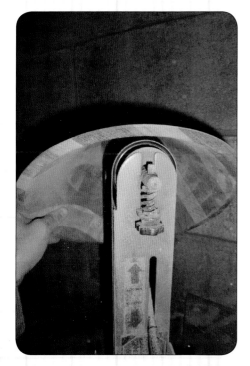

Step 11: Finishing Touches

Once the bowl is smooth, wipe it down with a wet cloth to remove any dust particles. Let it dry, then apply a one to three coats of varnish. Smooth out/sand with a high grit sandpaper as necessary.

kitchen

173

Universal Knife Block

By strooom
(http://www.instructables.com/
id/Universal-Knife-Block-Design-
Martin-Robitsch/)

Martin Robitsch designed a knife block like this one, and I immediately loved it. Because it is quite expensive, but not too hard to make one yourself, I decided to contribute another Instructable.

Materials

- 4 pieces of 255 mm × 140mm × 9 mm in nice solid wood (I used oak), these will be the sides of the box
- 1 piece of 130mm × 130mm × 8 mm. This will be the bottom and invisible, so it can be MDF or plywood.
- Around 2,000 bamboo skewers, 25 cm long

Other

- Wood glue
- Wood oil

Tools

- Saw (only needed if you need to cut the five pieces yourself)
- Sander. Ideally, you want a belt sander (I use the Bosch PBS 7 AE) for rough sanding and an orbital sander (I use Bosch GSS 280 AVE) for finishing.
- Clamps
- Router (optional, I use Bosch POF 800 ACE)

Effort: This takes about half a day. The cost is about $30. The Bamboo skewers I bought were $1.13 for 100 pieces. You could modify the dimensions if you want to; I just made it to the size of some oak I had left over, and the final result

is about the right size for three to six knives.

Step 1: Assembling the Box

The hardest part is gluing the box together. It may seem simple, but it is difficult to glue five pieces together, keeping right angles everywhere. So I decided to help you with some step by step advice:

1. Put one side on a flat surface.
2. Glue the bottom on top of it. Align the bottom and one corner (in my pictures I aligned the bottom right corner).
3. Glue one extra side at the opposite corner (so I added a side to the left).
4. Apply clamps and some weights (I often use books).
5. Glue the remaining sides, one by one.
6. Finish by applying a bit of glue to all inner joints with your finger.

Ideally, the side will stick out just a little on all four sides. That's okay (better than being too small). This excess will

175

be removed in the next step. Also, It is important to take your time—take it one part at a time and let it dry enough. (My glue takes about thirty minutes, but twenty-four hours for full hardening out). Patience is your friend here!

kitchen

Step 2: Trimming the Sides of the Box

On each side, the side panels will stick out a little bit. This could be removed with sanding it, but I always use a router for this. You need a straight router bit with a ball-bearing. This will trim the panels to be exactly flush with the adjacent sides. You could also do this with a sander, but it will take more time and will not be as precise.

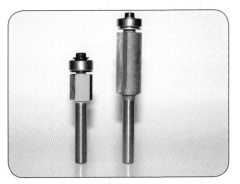

Step 3: Sanding the Box

Now, use a sander to finish the box; it should end up nicely square. All panels need to be clean and smooth. I usually start with the belt sander, using a grain of 80. Then I finish with the orbital sander, using a grain of 120 or 180.

Important tip: When using the belt-sander, keep the direction of the belt more or less parallel to the grain of the wood. If you sand it across the grain, you will get visible scratches, which are harder to remove. Always keep your belt sander moving over the piece; never let it rest in one position. If you keep it still, it may leave a groove that is, again, hard to remove.

kitcher

177

Step 4: Trimming the Bamboo Skewers

In my case, the bamboo skewers were 25 cm, but still they varied a bit in length. A little variation is no problem, but I still decided to adjust the ones that were sticking out too much. Here is how I did it:

1. Cut a piece of wood that fits in the box.
2. Then put the skewers in, with the tip pointing down. Because of the extra piece of wood, the sticks will stick out, and the longest ones will stick out the most.
3. Use the belt sander to carefully trim them down, so they are more even.

Note: The dust will fall in the box, so be careful when you remove the sticks, as some sawdust will fall out.

Remove the temporary piece of wood at the bottom of the box. If it is hard to shake it out, put in a screw so you can pull it out.

Step 5: Surface Finishing the Box

Oil the box, or use any other finishing of your liking. I like oil. I think if the wood could talk, it would prefer the oil as well. In this case I used Skydd from IKEA. Actually, I don't like IKEA's consumerism: cheap, disposable, imported, mass-produced furniture, but I like to use parts of what they sell and make long-lasting products with them.

After applying the oil, I added four felt pads at the bottom, in order to not scratch any surface. I later put the knife block on.

kitchen

Step 6: Adding the Bamboo Skewers

Finally, add the bamboo skewers. Make sure they all go in nicely parallel to the length of the box. Admire your result!

kitchen

Test Tube Spice Rack

By Noah Weinstein (noahw)
(http://www.instructables.com/
id/Test-Tube-Spice-Rack/)

Here's a test tube spice rack that I made to hold all of my spices. I tried to improve upon previous test tube spice racks that I've seen by using a nice-looking piece of bamboo plywood and by using oversized O-rings to "float" the tubes in the rack and eliminate the base plate. Also, my kitchen is short on counter space, so moving the spices out of the cupboard and onto the wall was a bonus. I've got a lot of spices, so I made two of these racks, but the design would work well with just one or as many as you might need to hold all of your spices. Sorry I can't publish this as a full step-by-step Instructable since this was one of the few builds I've done where I didn't take pictures along the way, but I'll do my best to explain how I made it in the text below.

Step 1: Materials

- Plywood bamboo strip approximately 2" × 16"
- Glass 25mm × 150mm test tubes from Drillspot
- Size 10 cork stoppers to match test tubes from Mcmaster
- 22mm × 4mm rubber O-rings to match test tubes from Mcmaster
- Assorted spices
- Skinny measuring spoons from Lee Valley
- Screw hook to hold measuring spoons
- Mini L brackets
- Hanging hardware for plaster or drywall walls

Step 2: Tools

- Saw to cut wood
- Drill or drill press (better) to drill holes in wood and hang rack
- 1⅛" Forstner bit to make clean holes that are slightly larger than test tube diameter but smaller than the O-rings.

Step 3: Construction

Cut appropriately-sized strips of wood for your test tube rack. On a drill press, use a 1⅛" Forstner bit to create evenly spaced holes on the rack. Try to drill as straight as possible if you're using a hand drill. Slip the O-rings onto the test tubes, fill with spices, and insert cork stopper into the top.

Step 4: Installation

Hang the test tube rack onto the wall with small steel L brackets, using appropriate anchors or hardware for your specific wall type.

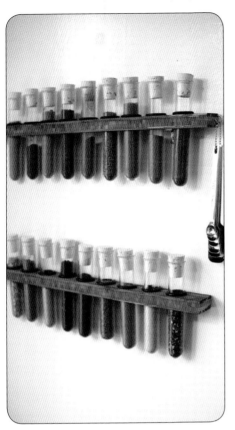

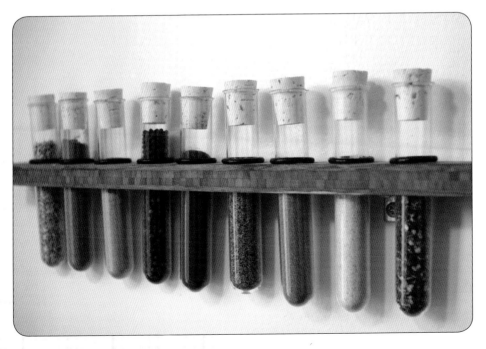

Shape-Shifting Wood Trivet

By BrittLiv
(http://www.instructables.com/
id/How-to-make-a-trivet-that-
can-change-the-shape/)

In this tutorial, I'm going to show you how to make a trivet that can change shape and be very easily stored. Being a student, space is very valuable in my kitchen. This trivet can be used for pans and pots of different sizes, without needing a huge amount of storage space.

By the way, this is a great gift for mums and grandmas.

Step 1: Basic Concept

I'm convinced that a picture is worth a thousand words. The image shows the concept of the trivet. Every piece can be turned freely around the neighboring pieces. You can, of course, connect more than one piece to another.

In one of my earlier tries, I've used round 2" × 2" lego plate to connect the pieces. I wondered whether the plastic

would be stable enough. However, no matter how hard I tried, I couldn't get it to melt, even by placing hot pots and casserole dishes on it. This is not too surprising, because wood is a pretty good insulator and the holes between the disks prevent heat accumulation. The connections weren't strong enough and it kept falling apart.

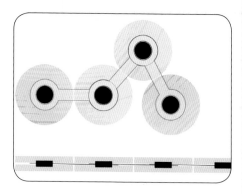

Step 2: Tools and Materials
Material

- Wooden disks (at least thirty; the height should be at least 6 mm). The size doesn't really matter, though they shouldn't be smaller then 3cm—the smaller they are the more you will need.
- Smaller wooden pieces, between 4 mm and 8 mm high and about 1.5 cm in diameter (I've used game pieces)
- Very strong glue
- A silicone sheet (to get the exact size follow this Instructable and then calculate it accordingly to your trivet)
- Sandpaper

Tools

- A drill press
- A Forstner drill bit (the diameter has to be the same as the smaller wood piece)
- A circle cutter (not really necessary but makes your life a whole lot easier)
- A box cutter

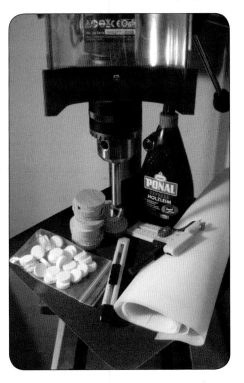

Step 3: Cut the Wooden Disks

I wasn't able to find wooden disks in the size I needed them (and I don't have a circular saw), so a friend offered to cut them (and I forced him to take photos). He used spruce, but you should get a hardwood because it's more durable, and softwood tends to get black when it's getting too hot.

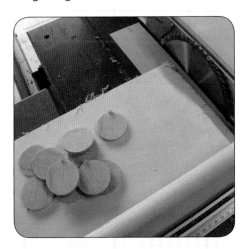

Step 4: Drill

It is very important that the hole is perfectly centered. You can either make a stencil out of paper or buy one. How deep you will have to drill depends on the height of your smaller wooden pieces. There should be enough space to connect the pieces but not *much* more or your trivet will get unstable. Remember that the center point is longer than the hole you are going to drill. Once you've adjusted the drill, don't change anything anymore and drill every piece in the exact same way.

Step 5: Connect the Pieces

To connect the pieces, you should make the connections out of a silicone sheet (if you can't find any, check out the last picture). The length between the two holes has to be the diameter of your wooden disks. The holes need to be a bit bigger than your small wooden pieces. I cut the outline with the circle and the box cutter and, when I was done with all the pieces, I cut the smaller holes.

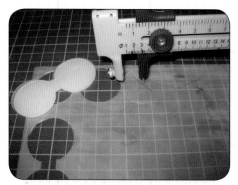

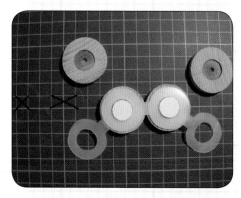

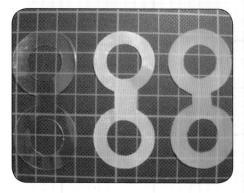

Step 6: Glue

Now you will have to glue the pieces that will connect your top and bottom part to your wooden disks. Start by gluing the smaller pieces into one of the bigger disks, lay out the connectors, and glue the second piece on top of it. Make sure that you don't glue the silicone to the wood by always trying to turn the pieces.

Step 7: What Now?

There are many ways to improve this concept. I tried using heat-resistant spray paint and it worked very well. Another way could be to use different types of wood to make it look more interesting or carve something into it. Maybe you can think of a way to use this concept for something different, e.g., jewelry or a toy.

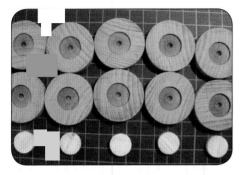

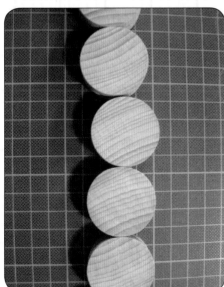

kitchen

185

shape-shifting wood trivet

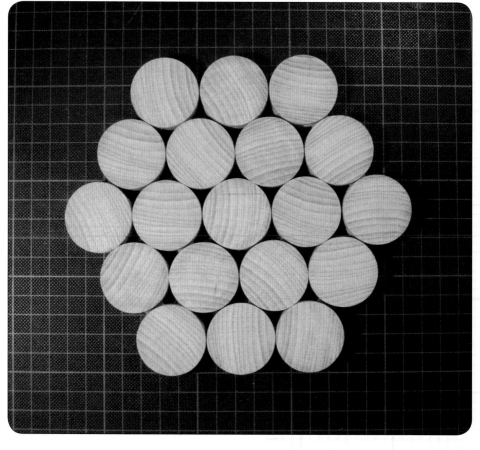

Section 7

Metal

This is an Instructible on how to make a coin into a tiny plane. It doesnt really have a purpose, but its quite a cool thing to make. I originally made it because a guy from college said he had one his grandad had made. I couldn't find one on here, or on the Internet, after having a quick look, so I just went for it. This is a step-by-step on how I made mine.

Note: If you notice that the back left fin of my miniature airplane is missing, you would be right. It broke off.

Step 1: Heat and Hammer Your Coin and then Bend It in Half

This first step is to choose your coin. I used a 10p piece for mine (about the same size as a quarter) because its silver in color, as opposed to the coppery color of a 2p. (This was purely for aesthetics. You could use any coin, but I'd recommend one about this size.)

I used a blowtorch to heat it up and hammer it out so it was flatter, slightly larger, and didn't have the pictures on either size. The unheated coin is a bit too thick, but be careful not to hammer it too thin. (In the picture is a 50p as well because I hadn't decided what coin I was going to use.)

Once it's hammered out, get the coin in a vise and bend it in half. It needs to be bent equally so both the sides meet level at the top. Once it's bent, heat and hammer it again so it's flat along the fold. You don't want a gap between the sides at the folded side, but it needs to have a gap at the sides that meet at the top. I forgot to take a picture of that bit and it's hard to explain, but it should make sense in the next step.

Step 2: Cut the Basic Shape and Unfold

Now that you've got your folded coin, you need to cut out the basic shape of the wings and tail. I put mine in a vise and used a jeweler's saw (very, very fine

metal

hacksaw) and cut down into the rounded side. You need to cut down, like I have in the picture, to mark out where you want the wings and the tail fins to be. You also need to cut out a wedge on the spine to make the upright tail fin.

Once you've done this, you need to "unfold" the wings and fins. This is where the whole thing about having the gap when their sides meet becomes important. I put mine so it was in a vise held by the spine, then used a chisel to bend out the wings. The picture may help here. You want to bend it out so that it looks roughly like a plane blank.

I mounted mine on a coin I had that has a cool design. I just cut a triangle shape, bent it up, and then super-glued the plane to it.

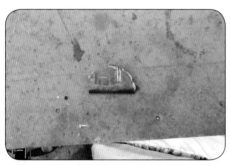

Step 3: Final Shaping and Mounting

This is the last stage. All that's left to do is to shape the blank into your desired plane shape. Mine is based roughly on a spitfire. I used the smallest files I could find to shape and polish it up a bit. I also hammered out the wings a bit more on mine so they were longer and thinner. You could spend forever doing this part using sandpaper, files, everything.

metal

I really enjoy turning scrap steel into objects that some people might find beautiful. The first picture shows a few of my pieces. I normally give my work away to friends or trade it for something completely different that, for example, a friend has created.

I have had some success using flat steel plate to make three-dimensional objects. In this Instructable, I will attempt to share the process so others might enjoy the experience, too. I don't intend to provide a pattern so you can make an identical object—I'm sure you will want something unique. I will simply outline the steps I took so you can see how easy it is.

Step 1: Inspiration and Planning

Inspiration can come from anywhere. Sometimes I can spend hours staring at image searches on the web. Sometimes I can walk into my workshop and just start making. This time I had a pair of old Chinese jars that I stole proportions from.

Working with flat steel, it helps to choose a design that can be broken down into a series of flat planes. In this case, I measured my old jars and drew a simple 3D sketch in AutoCAD. It looked okay, so I then drew all the faces on the one plane, trying to lay them out to minimize the required cutting. There were only three shapes: the hexagon base and two trapezoids making up the tapered sides and the shoulders.

Of course it's just as good to use a pen, a ruler, or even trace the outline of the object.

Since I could only print in A4, I decided to only print those three shapes—joined as they would be when making up the base and one side of the pot. I cut out the print with scissors and used that for my template.

Step 2: Marking Out

First find some steel. I prefer to work with free stuff that has been discarded. Chequer plate has a great texture. So does old rusty steel after it has been cleaned up a bit. In my example, I chose a sheet of steel about 1.5mm thick. In a

191

previous life, it had been used as a pallet to mix concrete on, so it took a lot of work to get it clean.

Work out the most efficient way of laying out the shapes needed and then, using your template, mark them out with chalk or soap stone.

Step 3: Cut Out

I use a thin cutting disc on my angle grinder. I see a lot of very high-tech cutting machines on Instructables these days, but sadly I don't have one. Simply cut out the outline and lightly score any line that will need to be folded.

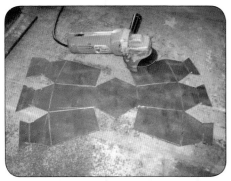

Step 4: Start Bending and Welding and Grinding and More Grinding

Using a vise, gloved hands, pliers, hammer, or whatever you can get hold of, gradually bend each fold one at a time until the sides are close enough to their final position for tacking.

I used a hammer to get joints tight enough to weld. When a joint is closed, tack it and move to the next. Close the joint and tack. And so on until the sides are all welded. Then bend the shoulders down and weld.

I left some steel at the tops of each shoulder piece in order to make a rim. I bent the rim pieces out as I formed the shoulders. These took some hammering to get them right for welding. (I'm actually not convinced the rim is necessary. I might just chop it off.)

If you are as rough a welder as me, you will now need to do a lot of grinding to make the thing look a bit neat. At this point, I also trimmed the rim.

metal

Step 5: Conclusion

There are many different ways to do a job like this. I have given a very brief and deliberately vague outline of the method I chose, hoping that this will be enough to inspire someone to get started on their own path.

metal

Make Your Own Rifle Cartridge Pen Blanks

By switch62
(http://www.instructables.com/
id/Make-your-own-Cartridge-
Pen-blanks/)

Having turned several wood and acrylic pens, I was looking at other unique types of pens. I found that you could get pen blanks made from bullet cartridges. I ordered some at a reasonable price ($2–$4) along with some rifle clips. I made pens out of the blanks, which look great. I also ordered a kit, which had all the parts and included the cartridge with a projectile (bullet) as the pen nib. Unfortunately I wrecked the cartridge (don't ask) and lost $20.

This got me to wondering if I could make my own. I was talking to a friend who has several rifles and uses reloaded bullets. I asked him where he buys the shells and projectiles and if they are expensive; he pointed me to a few gun shops. He also went one better and got me several different shells and projectiles through his mate who reloads the bullets.

I have now worked out how to make the cartridge blanks and the bullet kits. Though the bullet kits still have some kinks to be worked out.

So this Instructable shows how to make the cartridge blanks. I'll be using 308 cartridges, as they are the easiest to modify. They are just the right length and have the right neck diameter to match the pen nib. You can use other cartridges, but they must have a neck diameter to allow a 7mm tube to pass through.

Warning: This should only be done with new cartridges made for reloading or cartridges that have been fired (spent cartridges). *Do not* use an unfired bullet (live bullet). Trying to pull it apart may cause it to go off and *kill* or *injure* you or someone else.

Step 1: Bits and Pieces

- Some 308 Cartridges, new for reloading or used, no projectile or powder, fired or no primer
- 7mm pre-cut brass pen tubes or length of pen tubing
- Drill press with vise
- Drills imperial and metric
- Bench vise
- Soldering iron, 40 watts or more
- Wood lathe
- Pen mill
- ¼" bolt, 3" long and ¼" nut
- Thick CA glue
- Thin flux-cored solder
- Wet and dry sandpaper, various grades 400, 800, 1200
- Micro mesh pads, 1500 to 12000
- Brasso
- Maguires car polish

Optional
- Centering pen vise
- Pen turning mandrel
- Metal lathe
- Grinder with buffing/polishing wheels

- Rubber mallet
- Cutting oil
- Deburing tool

Step 2: Preparing the Cartridge

Depending on where you get your cartridges, they may or may not have a primer in the back. If you buy the cartridges new (for reloading), you should get them without a primer. If you get them from someone who reloads bullets or just spent rounds, the primer will probably still be there.

The primer should have a small dent in the center—this means it has gone off and should be safe. If there is no dent, leave it alone. Trying to remove an unfired primer may set it off and could cause you some harm.

If in doubt, leave it or take it to someone who knows what he or she is doing.

You can remove the primer by knocking it out with a long thin nail or rod, inserted from the neck of the cartridge (thinner part, where the projectile would be) to the center of the back. You should be able to tap it out gently with a hammer. No need to place it in a vise; either hold it in your hand or place it over a hole drilled in a piece of scrap wood.

Next, you need to drill a 7mm hole in the back of the cartridge. This hole needs to be exactly in the center of the cartridge, so you need to use a drill press or a lathe. A metal lathe would be ideal, but I don't have one (yet). I used my drill press and a centering vise that I use for drilling pen blanks. However you drill the hole, do it at a low speed. I set my drill press to its lowest speed of 500 rpm.

You could also use a vise with soft or V jaws. Another method might be a piece of wood with a hole drilled the same size as the cartridge. The wood should be cut down the middle. You can then clamp the bullet and wood halves in a drill press vise.

However you hold the cartridge, it needs to be in line with the drill bit and centered. I get it on center by using a smaller drill bit that just fits into the hole for the primer. With the drill press off, I nudge the vise until the drill bit goes smoothly into the hole without catching in the sides. I then clamp the vise in position, recheck, and put in the 7mm drill bit.

I then drill the 7mm hole into the cartridge. I use some cutting oil placed into the primer hole; this helps the drill bit to cut the brass smoothly. If you don't have cutting oil, just use some light oil or motor oil—you may get a little smoke with these. When drilling, don't do it in one shot. Drill a little at a time and allow any swaf to clear the hole; add more oil if needed. There is about 5mm of brass to drill through.

The next step is to clean the cartridge with degreaser or turpentine to remove the oil and any dirt. Once clean, use some 400-grit sandpaper rolled into a tube or wrapped around a rod, dowel, or drill bit to clean and roughen the inside of the cartridge neck. The inside of the neck should be a shiny brass color.

metal

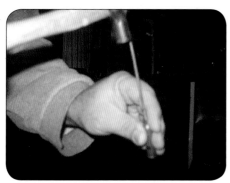

Step 3: Tube Preparation

Get a 7mm brass tube that's used for making pens. I used a tube from a Slimline pen kit, which was just a little longer than the cartridge. You can also get longer lengths of 7mm pen tubing; just cut a length about 5mm longer than the cartridge. Remove any burrs from the outside and inside of the cut tube.

Square off one end of the tube with a 7mm pen mill. You can do it by hand as the brass tube is thin and soft. Don't

metal

remove too much or the tube will be too short. Roughen the outside of the tube at each end with some 400- to 800-grit sandpaper.

Wrap some tape around the unsquared end of the tube. The tape should be enough to pass through the neck of the cartridge without any slack. It should be a firm fit but not tight. The edge of the tape should be about 3 mm from the open end of the neck. I used two to two-and-a-half layers of electrical tape. I then used clear sticky tape for the final fit, as it's much thinner. You may have to do some adjustments for each blank because neck diameter may vary slightly.

Step 4: Gluing and Soldering

Insert the 7mm tube into the cartridge from the neck, squared end first. Push it all the way through so the tube sticks out the back of the cartridge. Then push it back up to test that the tape centers the tube in the neck of the cartridge. If not, add some more tape to one side or the other.

Now, push the tube so it sticks out the back of the cartridge. Put some thick CA glue (super glue) on the end of the tube about 3mm back from the edge of the tube. Then push the tube back in until it is flush with the back of the cartridge. You should be able to make adjustments using the other end of the tube. There should not be any excess glue on the back of the cartridge. If there is, you can carefully scrape it off after it sets. Wait until the CA sets or use some accelerator.

Once the glue sets, we need to solder the other end. You need a soldering iron (+40 watt) and some thin electronics solder (flux-cored solder). I used my portable gas soldering iron with the large tip.

To hold the cartridge, I clamped a 3" long ¼" bolt into a bench vise and put a ¼" nut down at the bottom of the thread. I then put the cartridge over the bolt, neck end up. This gives support without drawing heat from the soldering process. The cartridge may want to rotate on the bolt when you apply the soldering iron; this may be useful if your iron can't heat the tube and the neck all the way around. You can just "walk" the soldering iron tip around the tube. Otherwise, some tape at the bottom should hold it long enough.

Place the tip of the hot soldering iron so that it touches both the cartridge and the tube and heat them until the solder melts when you touch it to the 7mm brass tube. Apply the solder only to the 7mm tube—you don't want

any solder on the outside of the neck. Then you should be able to apply solder all the way around. Don't use too much solder, as it will overflow onto the cartridge. Also, don't let it heat up too much, because the tape on the tube will start to melt and try to exit through the solder. The solder should flow and fill the gap between the tubes.

Once it has all cooled, take the cartridge off the bolt and sand or file the 7mm tube until it is almost flush with the cartridge neck. If you got any solder on the outside of the cartridge, use some 800-grit sandpaper to sand off the solder. Don't worry about the scratches as they will be polished out. Use the pen mill to square off the neck end. Again, you can do it by hand as the brass and solder are soft, just don't remove too much. Stop when the 7mm tube, solder, and cartridge neck are flat and shiny all the way around. Don't worry about any voids in the solder.

Step 5: Polishing

Now, you need to polish the cartridges. You can use Brasso by hand, but that may be a long and difficult process. If you have a grinder with buffing wheels, you can polish them like you would any piece of metal. I used my lathe and pen mandrel to polish the cartridges.

I placed the cartridges on the pen mandrel separated with 7mm pen bushings. I then used finer and finer grits of wet and dry sandpaper. I use the sandpaper wet. I start with 400 or 800 depending on how bad the surface of the cartridge is. I then go through the grits 400, 800, and 1200 and then the nine micro mesh pads 1500 - 12000. After each grit, I stop the lathe and sand along (horizontally) the cartridges all the way around, turning the lathe slowly by hand. This breaks up the circular scratches left when sanding on the lathe. I also wipe off excess water and grit each time.

After the sanding, I use brasso on a small piece of folded paper towel. Then, I wipe off and polish with an other piece of clean towel. I may do this two or three times until the cartridges are very shiny. I then apply some Maguires car polish to seal the brass; otherwise you'll get instant tarnish as soon as you touch the brass.

Apply the polish with some folded paper towel and then wipe off. Using another paper towel, pinch the paper towel around the cartridge to create some friction to set the polish. I do this twice.

Step 6: Make a pen

You can now use the cartridges to make pens using Slimline, Streamline, and Comfort 7mm pen components or kits. You can use two cartridges back to back to form a pen. One cartridge at the bottom and a wood or acrylic top. Camo-patterned acrylics go great with the bullet/gun theme.

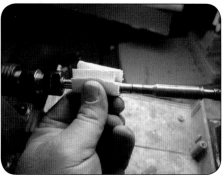

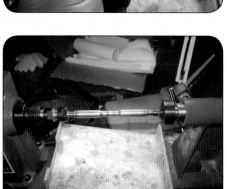

metal

I had just finished building a metal casting furnace and needed to make a Valentine's Day present for my wife. I found a similar project by Kiteman and decided to translate it into cast aluminum. I used a technique called lost foam casting, which involves pouring molten metal directly on a pattern made out of foam. The foam vaporizes and the metal fills the void, creating the casting. I hadn't tried it before but it's supposed to be fast and easy and involves fire. Who doesn't like that?

Step 1: Cutting the Pattern

First, you need a pattern of what you want to cast. You will need two hearts. Mine are about 5" tall and ¾" thick. Start with a piece of foam insulation. You want the pink or blue stuff that they sell at the hardware store. It's possible to use white beadboard, but it's crumbly and won't give as good of a resolution.

I cut out my heart patterns on a CNC router. You certainly don't need to use a CNC router to make your pattern. A saw, knife, file, etc. will do just fine. I cut out the heart in two pieces and glued them together. Make sure that you add two sprues off the top of the heart. This is where the aluminum will enter and exit the mold. It took about twenty minutes to cut each piece. The ridges in the pattern are because I cut it out at a low resolution. I was too impatient to wait longer for a smoother cut and I thought that they looked interesting.

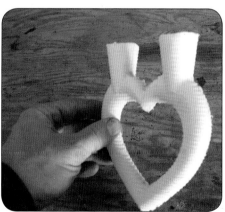

Step 2: Preparing to Cast

Now that you have your patterns, it's time to fire up the foundry. If you don't have a metal casting set up, you can find instructions for building one on Instructables or there is also an excellent forum/community of backyard metalcasters located at backyardmetalcasting.com/forums. I found them very helpful in getting me going with an inexpensive (runs off of waste vegetable oil), home-built foundry.

You can do lost-foam casting in a number of ways. I chose to just bury my pattern in loose sand. This is the easiest and most immediate method, but it gives you a grainy surface from the sand. I knew I was going to add some finishing to my castings so I didn't mind. I sifted regular play sand into an old soup pot and buried the first heart up to the top of the sprues. Then I took a short can with the top and bottom removed and put it around the entry side. The can acts as a collar to retain the metal and gives you an extra supply to help fill the mold as you are pouring. You also don't have to be quite as precise as you pour.

Step 3: Pouring

I guess it's time to mention that pouring molten metal can be exceedingly dangerous. Please take the time to research it thoroughly and use appropriate safety gear. You do not want to drop a crucible of liquid metal on your foot. I don't know what nasty chemicals are released when you vaporize foam, but I would strongly recommend pouring outside and wearing a respirator with organic vapor cartridges in addition to your other safety gear. Once your furnace is heated up and glowing orange, melt some aluminum in the crucible. Make sure you have plenty melted; you don't want to run out in the middle of a pour. My hearts took about 1 pound each with the sprues and excess. Have the pot with your mold on the ground near the furnace and all of your tools ready. When you pour the casting fill the metal collar and don't stop pouring until you see a puddle of metal coming out the other side. There will be some smoke and fire, but you don't want to hesitate in your pour or the metal can freeze up and the mold won't fill completely. Wait about five minutes after the pour to pull the casting out of the sand. You want to be sure it's nice and hard.

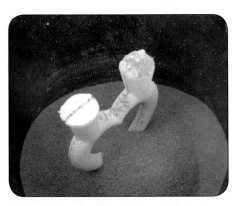

metal

go ahead and cast the second heart the same way you did the first.

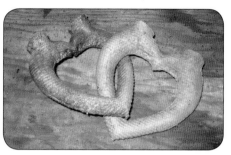

Step 5: Finishing

Now it's just a matter of removing the sprues and finishing the surface of the hearts the way you like. I used a saw to cut them off as close to the top of the hearts as I could. Be careful not to cut too much off. Next, I used a grinder to rough shape the tops. I used a file to do the final shaping and to smooth the surface somewhat. I wanted to leave the ridges in the hearts but also have them be smooth enough that they invite you to handle them. Finally, I used 120-grit sandpaper to take out the file marks and 600-grit to get the final finish. This was my first real CNC project and my first casting. I was very pleased with the result, and my wife liked her present, too.

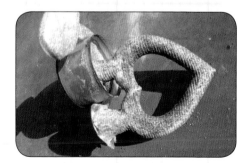

Step 4: The Second Pour

After the first casting has cooled enough to handle, cut the sprues off with a hacksaw or Sawzall. Cut the second heart and insert the casting so that they are linked like a chain. Glue the foam heart back together. As you bury the foam this time, float the first casting in the sand parallel to the bottom so that it doesn't touch the pattern. Then

metal

205

How to Make a Metal Rose

By Michael Downard and Ryan Downard (Downard Works)

(http://www.instructables.com/id/How-to-Make-a-Metal-Rose/)

The first thing you want to do when making a metal rose is make sure you have everything you will need to complete the project.

Materials

- Scrap or non-scrap metal
- A metal rod

Tools

- Angle grinder with cutting and grinding wheels
- Pliers (needle-nose preferably)
- Bench vice
- Arc welder with welding rods
- Propane torch with propane
- Drill press and drill bits
- A marking tool (sharpie, chalk, wax pencil, etc.)
- A ruler
- Safety gear
- Plasma cutter (optional)

Disclaimer: Any one who is injured in the process of making this project is responsible for his or her own injury. We are in no way responsible for any injury that may occur while building this. Proceed at your own risk.

Step 1: Cutting Out the Circles

You will need to cut out three circles from your scrap metal. First, you need to mark the circles on the scrap metal, using a stencil to trace your circles—either a paint can or a roll of tape or anything with a flat edge that is round. After you have your circles drawn, you then proceed to cut them out. Using either a plasma torch or an angle grinder, cut out the circles as round as you can. You will end up with three similar disks. Don't worry about cleaning up the edges; that will come later.

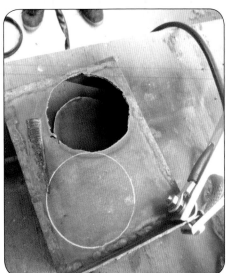

Step 2: Measuring and Cutting the Petals

For this step, you will need your ruler and angle grinder (or plasma torch). First you must find five points on the perimeter of the disk that are evenly spaced. You can do this several ways. Either take measurements and mark your points, or you could draw a star with the points touching the edge of the disk until it looks right. Either way you choose to do it, you will end up with five marks on the edge of the disk. Now you will draw them all to the middle of the circle until they meet at one point. This means it's time for cutting. When you're cutting the petals into the disk, be sure not to cut all the way down the line—there needs to be enough room for the hole that will be drilled though it.

Step 3: Clean Up the Edges

Now that we have the petals cut in, it's time to clean up the edges of the disk and to finish shaping the petals. For this you will need your angle grinder with the grinding and cutting disk. Be sure that the cuts are straight and all the way though the petals. Run the grinder over the surface of the petal disk repeatedly until it is smooth or shiny. Once the disk is smooth, round the sharp corners of the petals. This will make it safer and give it a more realistic petal look. Don't rush yourself on this step. How well you smooth the petals and round the corners will determine the look of the final product.

metal

way past the previous cut. Remember to check that each weld is a good one before continuing onto the next one.

Step 4: Drilling and Welding

Now we will begin the process of attaching the petals to the stem. For this you will need a drill press and an arc welder. First, make sure the place is marked where you need to drill the hole. When drilling the hole, be sure to not use your hand to hold it. Use pliers or a vice or something. If it starts spinning on the drill bit, it will slice your hand up. Also be sure to drill a small hole to start the process. Then work your way up in drill bit sizes until you have the size hole you want.

Once all three holes are drilled, take it to the welder. You will weld them from the top of the petals, so the next set of petals will sit on the previous weld. This is all the spacing that you will need for it to look good. Be sure to weld the petals so the cuts don't line up, or else it wont look like a rose when it's finished. A good rule of thumb is to rotate the next disk so the cuts are one third of the

Step 5: Heating and Shaping

Now it's time for the final step. For this you will need a propane torch and pliers. Heat the petals so that they are red hot. Be sure not to burn yourself on them; never reach over the top of them. They must be bent in a pattern or else they wont look right. One side of the petal should lie on the inside of another while the other half of the petal is covering the one next to it. Keep the top petals tight so the other petals can be folded up with enough room. It will take several heatings to bend all the petals. Once you're done folding the petals up, get creative with them. Organic things are never symmetrical. After you're happy with your new rose, clean out the flakes of metal from the inside and quench the metal by spraying it with the water hose. The rest is up to you. You can paint it or leave it as is. You could even make a vine of them. Turn them into art. Like this gate for instance.

metal

209

CONVERSION TABLES

One person's inch is another person's centimeter. Instructables projects come from all over the world, so here's a handy reference guide that will help keep your project on track.

Measurement								
	1 Millimeter	1 Centimeter	1 Meter	1 Inch	1 Foot	1 Yard	1 Mile	1 Kilometer
Millimeter	1	10	1,000	25.4	304.8	—	—	—
Centimeter	0.1	1	100	2.54	30.48	91.44	—	—
Meter	0.001	0.01	1	0.025	0.305	0.91	—	1,000
Inch	0.04	0.39	39.37	1	12	36	—	—
Foot	0.003	0.03	3.28	0.083	1	3	—	—
Yard	—	0.0109	1.09	0.28	033	1	—	—
Mile	—	—	—	—	—	—	1	0.62
Kilometer	—	—	1,000	—	—	—	1.609	1

Volume									
	1 Milliliter	1 Liter	1 Cubic Meter	1 Teaspoon	1 Tablespoon	1 Fluid Ounce	1 Cup	1 Pint	1 Quart	1 Gallon
Milliliter	1	1,000	—	4.9	14.8	29.6	—	—	—	—
Liter	0.001	1	1,000	0.005	0.015	0.03	0.24	0.47	0.95	3.79
Cubic Meter	—	0.001	1	—	—	—	—	—	—	0.004
Teaspoon	0.2	202.9	—	1	3	6	48	—	—	—
Tablespoon	0.068	67.6	—	0.33	1	2	16	32	—	—
Fluid Ounce	0.034	33.8	—	0.167	0.5	1	8	16	32	—
Cup	0.004	4.23	—	0.02	0.0625	0.125	1	2	4	16
Pint	0.002	2.11	—	0.01	0.03	0.06	05	1	2	8
Quart	0.001	1.06	—	0.005	0.016	0.03	0.25	.05	1	4
Gallon	—	0.26	264.17	0.001	0.004	0.008	0.0625	0.125	0.25	1

conversion tables

Mass and Weight						
	1 Gram	1 Kilogram	1 Metric Ton	1 Ounce	1 Pound	1 Short Ton
Gram	1	1,000	—	28.35	—	—
Kilogram	0.001	1	1,000	0.028	0.454	—
Metric Ton	—	0.001	1	—	—	0.907
Ounce	0.035	35.27	—	1	16	—
Pound	0.002	2.2	—	0.0625	1	2,000
Short Ton	—	0.001	1.1	—	—	1

Speed		
	1 Mile per hour	1 Kilometer per hour
Miles per hour	1	0.62
Kilometers per hour	1.61	1

Temperature		
	Fahrenheit (°F)	Celsius (°C)
Fahrenheit	—	(°C x 1.8) + 32
Celsius	(°F − 32) / 1.8	—